Comprehension and Literature

Jeanne McLain Harms

University of Northern Iowa

K|H
KENDALL/HUNT
PUBLISHING COMPANY
Dubuque, Iowa

Lyndon W. Searfoss, *Consulting Editor*
Mildred L. Middleton, *Language Arts Consultant*

Reviewers
State of Iowa Language Arts Committee
Sarah Hudelson—Arizona State University

Photographs by
Roger A. Kueter and Gary Braman, University of Northern Iowa

Copyright © 1982 by Kendall/Hunt Publishing Company

Library of Congress Catalog Card Number: 81–86476

ISBN 0–8403–2667–X

Printed in the United States of America

C   402667   01

Contents

Preface

This book deals with how children in kindergarten through grade eight develop comprehension abilities (viewing, listening, and reading) through literature. The cognitive and affective aspects of the different levels of comprehension and the representative tasks associated with each level are presented. For each level of comprehension, examples of the children's responses, based on child development theory, are related to the representative tasks and to experiences with literature. All of the examples given of children's experiences with the comprehension process and literature actually happened. When professionally advisable, the author has cited children and teachers for their contributions. Activities and materials for the development of comprehension abilities through literature experiences are supplied for each category. The suggestions include teacher-presented activities and independent learning centers. Many bibliographies of materials are included in the appendices.

The book is an outgrowth of the work of the Language Arts Curriculum Development Committee, appointed by the State Department of Public Instruction of Iowa to revise the curriculum development materials published in 1968. The present committee plans to publish a rationale for curriculum development as well as books on comprehension and composition. A subcommittee on comprehension (Richard Zbaracki, Iowa State University; Mildred Middleton, Cedar Rapids Community Schools; and the author) developed a model and a list of representative tasks. The author then related the model and tasks to classroom activities and materials.

Several purposes are envisioned for this book. First and foremost, it is designed to serve as a reference for classroom teachers and school curriculum development committees and as a basis for school inservice programs. The suggestions can be used to supplement existing reading and language programs or can serve as a guide for revision. The book can also be used in university workshops and seminars on reading and language arts as well as to supplement texts in reading and language arts methods courses and language curriculum development courses.

Many people made contributions to this book. The resources of the Youth Collection of the University of Northern Iowa and the fine services of its librarians, Arlene Ruthenberg and Lucille Lettrow, have been invaluable to me. The faculty of the Price Laboratory School at UNI offered my students and me opportunities to develop many language and literature experiences for children. Mildred Middleton and my colleagues, Max Hosier and Ned Ratekin, read the manuscript and made helpful suggestions. The comments of other members of the Language Arts Curriculum Development Committee were also greatly appreciated. Discussions about the manuscript with teachers in the Cedar Rapids Community Schools, the Des Moines Independent School District, and the West Des Moines Schools yielded many valuable insights.

Grateful acknowledgment is given to Cheryl Smith for editorial assistance, Barbara Kueter for typing the manuscript, and Roger Kueter and Gary Braman for the photographs.

Introduction

Comprehension is a complex thinking process that involves the receptive language arts: viewing, listening, and reading. In comprehending ideas expressed through a symbol system, people's responses are influenced by their thinking strategies, their understanding of language, and experiences with their culture. The process of comprehension includes knowing and feeling, or cognitive and affective tasks.[1]

Several levels of thinking make up the comprehension process, a model of which is presented in Figure 1. The nature of the work of literature, the purposes of the audience, as well as the audience's level of intellectual and social-emotional development, knowledge of language, and background of experiences are all factors which will determine the level of the comprehension process at which the audience will perform. Representative tasks for each level are as follows:

Attention

I. Willingness to view, listen, and read
    A. Anticipates a sequence of ideas and elements of a work
    B. Shows a sensitivity to what others say; attends to other points of view and different ways of expressing ideas
    C. Relates ideas of others to own ideas
    D. Understands that books and other media are concerned with people, places, things, and ideas

Model of Comprehension Process*

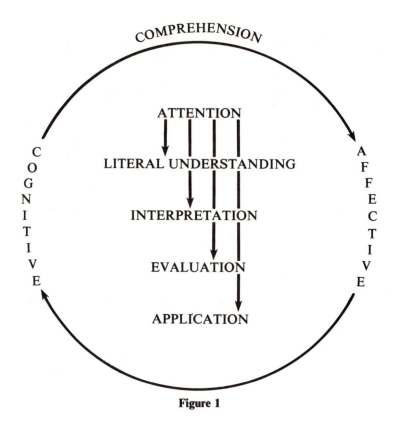

Figure 1

*Dr. James Davis assisted the author in developing the model.

II. Awareness of thought-symbol relationships
   A. Understands that nonverbal language, speech, and print are used for communication
   B. Matches print to speech
   C. Matches intonation to punctuation
   D. Recognizes clues to pronunciation and meaning (phonetic, morphemic, syntactic, semantic)
   E. Uses word recognition skills
   F. Recognizes print patterns
      1. Progresses left to right, top to bottom, front to back
      2. Skims and scans
      3. Follows paragraph divisions, topics, and subtopics

Literal Understanding

I. Cognitive tasks
   A. Notes elements, such as
      1. Sequence of ideas
      2. Direct statements of characters and setting
      3. Description of characters and statements of idea development
      4. Supporting details of main idea or theme
      5. Point of view of storyteller
      6. Imagery
      7. Sound elements of language
   B. Notes features or parts of specific types of stories, such as humorous stories and fables
   C. Recognizes organizational patterns
II. Affective tasks
   A. Responds emotionally to elements and features in light of personal experiences
   B. Empathizes with certain characters and events
   C. Relates work to personal experiences and knowledge of the world
   D. Examines personal feelings evoked by a work
   E. Listens to others' responses to a work

Interpretation

I. Cognitive tasks
   A. Understands elements, such as
      1. Sequence of ideas
      2. Character delineation
      3. Character and idea development
      4. Supporting details of a main idea or theme
      5. Different plot devices
      6. Point of view of storyteller
      7. Mood

        8. Imagery
        9. Figurative language
      10. Sound elements of language
      11. Style
  B. Recognizes characteristics of different types of literature
  C. Relates elements to one another
      1. Relates characters and actions to plot
      2. Predicts outcomes and forms conclusions
      3. Understands literary elements as clues to meaning
      4. Relates ideas to each other
      5. Recognizes organizational patterns
  D. Considers elements and parts as they relate to the meaning of the whole work
  E. Detects relationships between characters as reflections of meaning
  F. Understands the contributions of different types of literature to understanding an idea or a concept
  G. Sees different levels of meaning in a work
  H. Recognizes intention of author
II. Affective tasks
  A. Relates work to personal experiences and knowledge of the world
  B. Understands values within a work
  C. Relates ideas and values in a work to ideas and values in other works

Evaluation

I. Cognitive tasks
  A. Establishes criteria as means to judge a work
      1. Establishes criteria of form
      2. Establishes criteria of content
  B. Compares work to others of its kind
II. Affective tasks
  A. Uses own value system to judge work
  B. Re-examines own responses to work in light of responses of others

Application

I. Cognitive tasks
  A. Generalizes from content to build a base for problem-solving strategies
  B. Generalizes from experiences with work(s) to develop effective techniques of expression
II. Affective tasks
  A. Relates values identified in work to own and those of others
  B. Understands literature as a method of stating and exploring values; uses literature as a means to explore values
  C. Respects place of literature as a means to understanding

D. Respects others' right to read
E. Relates literature to other subjects and situations in life
F. Moves from a work to creative experiences

The levels of comprehension increase in difficulty from attention to application, with each level serving as a foundation for the next. Much of young children's comprehension involves the attention tasks. Older students engage in attention and then move on to more complex tasks. Some students do not progress in school language arts programs because they are not able to attend. The tasks of literal understanding deal with ideas that are expressed explicitly by the author. With a sufficient background of experiences, most children in school are able to perform these tasks. As children mature and have experiences with language and literature, they are able to engage in tasks on the interpretation level. These tasks involve manipulating explicit ideas to see relationships and understand implicit ideas. To function on the evaluation level, students need to establish criteria to judge works. This is accomplished through many experiences with works of literature and the development of a personal value system. The evaluation process enables students to gain an appreciation of excellence in literature.

On each of the levels, communication can come full circle. Comprehension activities can lead naturally to composition experiences. After gaining an understanding of ideas, students can express their reactions, verbally or through art, music, drama, or dance. On the application level, students use their experiences from all the preceding levels of comprehension to generate problem-solving strategies, develop effective techniques of expression, and explore and discover new ideas and relationships. Important affective tasks on this level are appreciating the place of literature in people's lives, understanding and using literature as a method of exploring and stating values, and respecting others' right to read.

The following chapters of this book deal with children's responses to comprehension tasks on the different levels and present learning activities to foster the abilities to perform these tasks.

The development of the comprehension process is influenced by experiences with language and literature. Students who have memorable experiences with literature are more willing to respond, remember, and manipulate ideas from works. They can then advance to more demanding tasks, such as evaluation and application. During this development process, students should be exposed to high-quality literature which is related to their interests. Good literature is memorable. It is characterized by carefully developed characters, plots, and ideas and interesting language patterns and styles.[2]

The behavior of teachers is crucial in the development of the comprehension process. Teachers must be knowledgeable about literature and the intellectual and emotional development and interests of their students. They must know how to present literature in an appealing way and how to react constructively to students' responses to literature. The behavior of teachers in learning situations can influence students' habits of viewing, listening, and reading and their development of literary interests, appreciation, and tastes.

In selecting comprehension experiences, teachers need to consider tasks from the interpretation and evaluation levels as well as tasks from the lower levels. They must recognize how literary elements, such as characterization and plot devices, and their interrelationships contribute to a work of high quality. They should also be aware of how different types of literature contribute to the understanding of an idea or concept. Recognizing the intention of authors is another important consideration that enables teachers to give more effective presentations of works. Teachers must bring together an understanding of the needs of their students and of the criteria of fine literature to judiciously select works for comprehension experiences.

Reading aloud different types of literature to students can establish the groundwork for much language learning as well as a basis for communication between teachers and their students. McCormick's summary of research on the benefits of reading aloud to children indicates that children's language growth is significantly affected. Their vocabulary knowledge and reading comprehension are improved.[3] Hearing literature read aloud influences reading interests and the quality of language development. Discussing the ideas in works which have been read aloud provides teachers and children with an opportunity to know and understand each other in a more comfortable sense. Literature offers people the opportunity to know about being human.

Discussion of works which students have encountered in viewing, listening, or reading experiences can benefit in many ways. Children's responses to ideas found in stories and poems are valuable sources of diagnostic teaching. How children respond to ideas in whole units of language serves as a valuable source of information about their intellectual and socio-emotional development, their past experiences with language and literature, and their interests. This information can assist teachers in providing effective learning experiences for their students.

In guiding discussions, teachers can ask broad questions that encourage children to consider the work as a whole. Broad questions allow children to recall what they were able to comprehend and what they thought was important and interesting. Examples of this type of question are, What did you like about the story (or poem)? How do you feel about the story (or poem)? Rapid-fire questioning, using who, what, when, and where questions, often detracts from students' understanding and appreciating literature and from moving to higher levels of comprehension tasks.

Discussions allow teachers opportunities to ask children to further clarify responses and to help them process and recall ideas. Discussions are also an alternative for written assignments. Many children find writing out answers a stumbling block to meaningful experiences with literature and language.

Evaluation of children's comprehension abilities has tended to deal in a fragmented way with lower-level comprehension skills and with limited units of language. Children's responses to tasks on the higher levels of comprehension, to larger units of language, and to different types of literature need to be included in evaluation. Interviews, discussions, and children's records of their involvement with literature and comprehension tasks will assist teachers in ascertaining what children are reading (the quality and the types of literature), what they are doing with the literature experiences (levels of comprehension tasks performed and composition activities engaged in), and what their plans are for further involvement in comprehension activities.

Notes

1. For further study of the comprehension process, see "Reading and Language," the December, 1977, issue of *Theory into Practice,* edited by Martha King, and *Teaching Reading Comprehension,* by William D. Page and Gay Su Pinnell. For an indepth discussion of comprehension based on the findings of psycholinguists, Frank Smith's book *Understanding Reading* is an excellent source. See the bibliography at the end of this chapter for complete citations.
2. Some suggested references of children's literature are Huck's *Children's Literature in the Elementary School,* Sutherland and Arbuthnot's *Children and Books,* and Glazer and Williams' *Introduction to Children's Literature.* See the bibliography at the end of this chapter for complete citations.
3. Sandra McCormick, "Should You Read Aloud to Your Children?" *Language Arts,* LIV (February, 1977), 139–43.

Bibliography

Glazer, Joan I., and Gurney Willians, III. *Introduction to Children's Literature.* New York: McGraw-Hill Book Company, 1979.

Huck, Charlotte S. *Children's Literature in the Elementary School.* 3rd ed. update. New York: Holt, Rinehart and Winston, 1979.

McCormick, Sandra. "Should You Read Aloud to Your Children?" *Language Arts,* LIV (February, 1977), 139–43.

Page, William D., and Gay Su Pinnell. *Teaching Reading Comprehension.* Urbana, Ill.: National Council of Teachers of English, 1979.

"Reading and Language." *Theory into Practice,* XVI (December, 1977).

Smith, Frank. *Understanding Reading.* 2d ed. New York: Holt, Rinehart and Winston, 1978.

Sutherland, Zena, and May Hill Arbuthnot. *Children and Books.* 5th ed. Glenview, Ill.: Scott, Foresman and Company, 1977.

Attention

For the users of language, the process of attending involves (1) being motivated to think and relate experiences to receptive language situations (viewing, listening, and reading) and (2) being aware of thought-symbol relationships (nonverbal, oral, and written). Representative characteristics of attending are as follows:

I. Willingness to view, listen, and read
  A. Anticipates a sequence of ideas and elements of work
  B. Shows sensitivity to what others have to say; attends to other points of view and different ways of conveying ideas
  C. Relates ideas of others to own ideas
  D. Understands that books and other media are concerned with people, places, things, and ideas
II. Awareness of thought-symbol relationships
  A. Understands that nonverbal language, speech, and print are used for communication
  B. Matches print to speech
  C. Matches intonation to punctuation
  D. Recognizes clues to pronunciation and meaning (phonetic, morphemic, syntactic, semantic)
  E. Uses word recognition skills
  F. Recognizes print patterns
    1. Progresses left to right, top to bottom, front to back
    2. Skims and scans
    3. Follows paragraph divisions, topics, and subtopics

Attending is used on all levels of language experience. Much of young children's comprehending is attending. Children who are more advanced in intellectual functioning and language acquisition use attending to initiate more complex comprehension processes.

Preschool Experiences

Experiences with literature offer very young children opportunities to respond to ideas presented by others. Two-year-old Wendell was attending as his mother retold Sendak's *Where the Wild Things Are*. Wendell excitedly called himself a monster and said, "I will eat you up." After acting out his ideas about a "wild thing," he hugged each of the three adults present.

Patty, as a three-year-old, also was listening for meaning when she found that the troll in a puppet show of *The Three Billy Goats Gruff* was fierce. She responded by standing up and saying, "I don't like that troll; I'm afraid," and ran to the back of the room to sit on an adult's lap.

Nina, at two years, discovered that stories have rhythm and repetition of phrases. Each night at bedtime she insisted that her father read Emberley's *Drummer Hoff* while she tapped out the rhythm on the bed with her arms and legs and chimed in with "but Drummer Hoff fired it off!" As she became more acquainted with the story, she marched about reciting parts of it. She was able to follow the patterns of the story and anticipate the elements.

After a group of preschool children had heard *Mr. Gumpy's Outing,* by Burningham, they indicated sensitivity to the character, Mr. Gumpy. They said they would want him for a friend because he was not cross with the animals for overturning the boat after he had warned them. Then he even invited them to tea.

Julie, three years old, was able to relate her own experiences to the story, *The Three Bears*. She was concerned about the little bear's broken chair and told her mother that two of her friends, an electrician and her doctor, could be asked to fix the chair. After making this suggestion several times, Julie told her mother that she did not want her to read the story any more if she was not going to ask these friends to fix the chair.

Preschool children attend from their point of view. In attending to the ideas in stories, they show sensitivity to the emotional elements and respond with body movements as well as verbal language. Sometimes their responses are surprising to adults, who may not understand that young children have difficulty reasoning logically through a sequence of ideas and distinguishing between fantasy and reality.

Very young children can begin to be aware of thought-symbol relationships. When eighteen-month-old Johnny rode with his mother in the car, he was given picture books to keep him occupied. He attended to the illustrations in the books and responded with simple speech, sometimes unintelligible, and gestures. As his language developed and he had more experiences with books, he increasingly was able to tell more elaborate sequences of ideas. By three years of age, Johnny knew that symbols and ideas were related. He proudly identified his and his sister's names, found that his name as well as three other relatives' names started with the same letter, and read traffic signs and words in advertisements and on cereal boxes. He was also watching the printed page as he was read to. His head and eye movements indicated that he was becoming aware of print patterns. When simple stories were read, Johnny, at four, wanted to follow along line by line with an envelope. Finally, one day he told his mother he wanted to read. As he read, his mother supplied the words he did not know.

Beginning Experiences in School

Much of the comprehension program in kindergarten and first grade centers on the process of attending. In our contemporary culture, many children beginning school have had more contact with television than they have had with parents and other caring adults. Therefore, these children have had few opportunities to respond to sequences of ideas that are meaningful to them and to become aware of thought-symbol relationships. To develop language abilities, children need consistent involvement in language experiences with others. Johnny, who was beginning to read before he went to school, was a member of a reading family. The adults in his life overtly showed their pleasure in his progress in language acquisition and his interest in books. They found time to read to him and to view selected television programs with him. Frequently, ideas derived from watching television were expanded. For example, when McCloskey's *Blueberries for Sal* was read on a children's program, Johnny asked questions about blueberry picking. Even though this experience was not possible, he and his mother found blueberries at the grocery store. The book was also checked out of the library along with *Make Way for Ducklings,* another book by the same author. These books were read many times, and Johnny's mother suggested them to relatives as gifts for Johnny's birthday.

Schools need to continually remind parents that the best way to prepare for their children's success in school is to involve themselves in their children's language experiences. Children benefit from having their parents watch and discuss television programs with them, converse about shared walks and visits to parks and museums, and share problems, such as being afraid of the dark or the bigger neighbor child who is not always kind.

Parents who read aloud to their young children are providing attending experiences with literature.

Children need opportunities to share interesting ideas from books with others.

Goodman suggests that beginning language programs in schools should center on building personal-social functions rather than skills and on whole units of language rather than fragments.[1] Programs that include a great deal of carefully selected literature and accompanying experiences allow children to learn about themselves, others, and the world in which they live and to use whole units of language. Programs emphasizing isolated word practice (flash cards and games), carefully controlled vocabulary and sentence patterns, letter-sound relationships studied apart from meaningful units, and stories with little content deny children the opportunities to gain insight into the usefulness of language. Language is a process; it is to be used.

Evaluation in beginning language programs needs to include observations of children's responses to ideas found through viewing, listening, and reading. Limited criteria for the evaluation of language abilities, such as naming the letters of the alphabet, identifying the sounds of letters, cutting with scissors, knowing colors, and coloring within lines, distract teachers from learning about children's understanding and use of language.

Teacher-Presented Activities

The attending experiences of young children in the elementary school are affected greatly by the behavior of their teachers. Because these children, for the most part, do not read independently and have not mastered the tools for using libraries, teachers need to assume the responsibility for finding and presenting literature to them. Experiences with literature can be presented to young children through books and other media, such as tapes, records, filmstrips, films, and television. These experiences can be presented directly by teachers, other adults, or children and in learning centers. It is important that teachers find many opportunities each day to read literature aloud to children. (Appendix A contains a list of recently published volumes for young children.)

Examples of fine literature can serve as models of language to children, who generally deal with language on a preconscious level. Children in kindergarten and first grade know a great deal about language but usually do not analyze elements in stories and poems or generalize about ideas found in literature. These attending experiences prepare children for more complex thinking experiences.

Young children in elementary school usually perceive experiences with literature as fun and interesting. Teachers, however, need to have a broader view of these experiences. Besides providing enjoyment, teachers should be striving to develop children's interest in and appreciation of fine literature, to expose them to different types of literature, to offer them examples of whole units of language, and to provide them with experiences with personal-social functions. Over 2,000 volumes are published annually for children. Teachers need to sort through this mass of publications to find material of interest to children and of high literary quality.

Through literature, children can find words and ideas that represent interesting experiences. Burningham, in the picture book *Would You Rather* . . . , chooses fun words and ideas that are meaningful to children. For example, "Would you rather . . . an elephant drank your bath water, an eagle stole your dinner, a pig tried on your clothes, or a hippo slept in your bed."[2] Many interesting words and sensory experiences are presented in Tresselt's *What Did You Leave Behind?* such as an experience with snow. "In you come, with snow inside your boots, soggy wet mittens and a cherry-red nose. Unwrap, unzip, undo, and there you are."[3]

Many types of literature need to be presented to young children. Both fanciful and realistic stories can deal with the concerns of children. Folk literature offers interesting patterns and sounds of language, characterization, events, and ideas. Both stories and poems need to be presented in a literature period.

Poetry offers as wide a range of content and emotional experiences as prose, though peotry is more intense. It presents children opportunities to attend to ideas and language in a new and fresh manner. The sound of language, imagery, and figurative language found in poetry give children a compelling invitation to attend and then to join in the language experience. It is amazing how quickly children can recite many poems from memory. As children listen to poems, they can chime in when they know the lines. Because of the concise way ideas are expressed in poems, they need to be reread many times.

Appendix B gives a selected bibliography of recently published volumes of poetry for children of all ages. Newer volumes are listed to acquaint teachers with recent trends in children's poetry. Contemporary poetry is characterized by being more childlike than childish; it deals more with ideas that are of particular interest to children. The wider range of content includes urban settings and minorities. Also, many different types of poetry, including experimental forms and adaptations of Oriental forms, are being published.

Children need many experiences in listening to literature being read aloud as whole units of language. These experiences can be the basis for their understanding such elements in literature as repetition and refrain, plot organization (patterns of three, surprise endings, cumulative tales, full circle, cause and effect), sensory awareness, and characterization. (Examples of these literary elements can be found in Appendix C.)

Literature experiences can provide children with ideas that can expand their understanding of themselves, others, and the world. In Yolen's *No Bath Tonight,* the grandmother helps the boy overcome his reluctance to take a bath by making "kid tea" and reading the leaves. The grandmother in *Albert's Toothache,* by Williams, also has a special understanding of children. Daniel, in Montresor's *Bedtime,* escapes into interesting, fanciful adventures to avoid bedtime until he finds a way to escape it. In *The Alligator Under the Bed,* by Nixon, Uncle Harry rescues Jill from her imagination and the alligator under her bed.

Fine literature read aloud by the teacher should be a primary motivation for children to attend. Reading aloud to children can be supplemented by using other media presentations, music, dramatizations and narrative pantomime, flannelboard stories, and the composition of stories and poems by the children themselves.

Media presentations. After a story is read to children, it can be presented through another medium. For example, the picture book *Time of Wonder,* by McCloskey, could be read and then followed by the film, which pans the pages of the book. Gerald McDermott's *Anansi the Spider* could be shared in book form before or after the film version is shown. Appendix D lists media sources.

In the case of children not accustomed to having stories read to them, a film, filmstrip, or tape of a televised program may serve to catch their attention initially so that their interest can be guided to books. Selected programs on educational television can be taped by schools and retained temporarily or permanently.

Music. Language and literature can be presented through music. Appendix E contains a list of song books and picture books based on songs. Children can listen and read along with tapes or records.

Flannelboard stories. Through flannelboard stories, children can extend their experiences anticipating sequences of ideas and elements of the story. Stories featuring characters with body parts that can be manipulated make appealing flannelboard presentations. For example, the red wings of Little Rabbit in the picture book *The Little Rabbit Who Wanted Red Wings,* by Bailey, can be put on and taken off the flannelboard. The tail of the fox in Hogrogian's *One Fine Day* can be taken off and put on as the story unfolds. Dandelion in Freeman's book by that name can be dressed and undressed as the plot develops. Appendix F contains a suggested list of books for flannelboard story experiences.

Narrative pantomime. Experiences with books can be extended to narrative pantomime. In narrative pantomime, all children in a group can respond bodily to the ideas attended in stories and poems. Heinig and Stillwell's book, *Creative Dramatics for the Classroom Teacher,* presents the principles underlying narrative pantomime, techniques for using this form of expression with children, and sources of materials.[4] Appendix G gives a list of stories suitable for use with narrative pantomime.

Stories and poems composed by children. Stories and poems that children have composed can serve as interesting attending experiences.[5] (Appendix H contains directions for poetry forms.) Children are often able to relate more closely to their own viewpoints than to those of adults. These compositions may be an individual child's efforts that have been dictated to another person or into a tape recorder and then transcribed and in some cases illustrated by the child. Stories and poems can also be composed by a group of children and then compiled into booklets. Picture story paper (18 inches by 12 inches) has lines and a blank space at the top of the sheet for illustrations. If sheets of picture story paper are arranged with a sheet of drawing paper on the outside and then stitched together down the middle before writing or transcribing is done, a book can easily be made. The outside sheet of drawing paper can serve as endpapers and can be glued to a cover of construction paper or wallpaper. Pages from large sample books of wallpaper are easy to use because they are flat and already cut.

Stories and poems composed by children can facilitate their interest in listening and reading.

Student-Assisted Activities

Older students can assist teachers in offering language experiences to young children. They can read aloud to children, present media experiences and flannelboard stories, and take children's dictation for stories and poems. For certain periods of the school schedule, older students can serve as aides in working with young children. Pairs, made up of an older student and a younger one, can be assigned to work together on a regular basis. Usually the teacher should suggest the experiences and materials. Before the student assistants begin to work, they need to be briefed about the interests and responses of young children. Older students need to understand that the stage of social-emotional and intellectual development of young children may cause them to respond in ways that differ from their own responses. For example, five-year-old girls may want to hold hands and sit close together with older boy students. Student assistants need to be prepared to interpret young children's responses that seem inappropriate, unreasonable, incorrect, or self-centered.

Older students can present many experiences with literature to younger children.

Independent Learning Centers

Learning centers can assist teachers in providing attending experiences for young children. To use the centers more effectively, teachers usually need to explain the activities and procedures to the students. Most of the experiences could be an extension of teacher-presented activities. For example, a new book in the library can be presented and then placed in the library center to be viewed and read or to be used with an accompanying tape. The specific centers the children use should be monitored by teachers or aides. Children need opportunities to share their experiences in the centers with the teacher and other children in the class. In Appendix I, suggestions for independent learning centers are given.

Some suggestions for using centers with young children are given below:

I. Viewing and reading centers
   A. Picture books for viewing and reading need to be available at all times.
   B. A center of newly published or newly acquired picture books can be developed.
   C. Collections of books that extend the experiences of children can be presented. These collections could include books about specific topics or concepts, such as seasons or holidays; books related to concepts from other content areas; or books by a particular author with information and letters from the author.
   D. Books with no text or minimal text can be viewed and then shared with others. Appendix J contains a list of books of this type.

A comfortable book center filled with interesting books can encourage children to attend.

  E. Easy-to-read books give experiences to children who are just beginning to read. Appendix K contains a list of these books.

  F. Dolls and puppets of characters in books can be manipulated as children view and read.

  G. Hats and costumes related to books can be worn during viewing and reading experiences.

  H. Books composed and illustrated by children can be developed into a center or as part of a center with related books.

II. Viewing and listening centers

Films, filmstrips, cassette tapes, records, and tapes of televised programs on literature can be used, possibly with assistance from an adult or older child.

III. Viewing, listening, and reading centers

  A. Tapes and records of the text of books, either commercially prepared or teacher-made, can be used in centers. Young children can learn much about reading by following along in books with a tape or record. Most of the suggestions in the section on viewing and reading can be used with tapes and records.

  B. Tapes and records of songs with accompanying picture books, charts, or sheets of the lyrics can form a center.

  C. Tapes and records can enhance the experience with poetry because it is an oral form. Poems on a specific topic or concept, such as snow, witches, or frogs, can be placed in booklets and used with an accompanying tape.

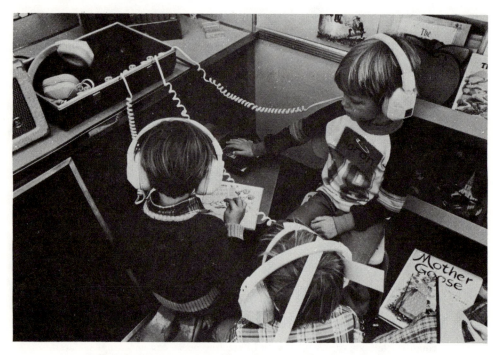

A listening center can provide many comprehension experiences.

    D. Flannelboard pieces can be displayed by children as they listen to tapes and records of stories or after they have read a story.

IV. Bookmaking center

The materials for making books can be set up in a center. The procedures for making a simple book are described in the section on "Teacher-Presented Activities," under the subtitle "Stories and poems composed by children." The materials needed are picture story paper, drawing paper, construction paper or wallpaper, darning needles, yarn, and glue.

Parent-Assisted Activities

Teachers can use conferences and newsletters to help parents become aware of and understand their children's language learning. Teachers can assist parents greatly in interpreting the responses that young children give when viewing, listening, and reading.

Parents need to be encouraged to take their children to the library for story hours and to select books to read aloud to them at home. A regularly scheduled time for sharing books is beneficial. The school can provide opportunities for children and their families to purchase paperbacks and accompanying records. Flannelboard stories that are well-known to children can be checked out at school and told at home to parents and siblings. (The pieces for the flannelboard stories might be listed on the container so that parents can make sure that all of the pieces are returned.) Stories and poems written by children can be sent home for them to share with their families. One kindergarten teacher does not send a child's composition home until she has discussed with the parents the nature of the child's responses and the value of sharing these stories and poems. Frequently, parents tell her that they did not know their child was capable of these responses.[6]

Conferences and newsletters provide an opportunity for parents to share with other parents their experiences in using books with young children. For example, Annabeth, a first grader, wore a T-shirt to school which she had received for Christmas. On the front was printed "We Can Read" and on the back, "Frog." Annabeth and her father had read Lobel's frog and toad books, with Annabeth taking the part of the frog and her father reading the part of the toad. He had a shirt with "Toad" printed on the back.[7]

An interesting program for parents' night would be to have parents share the reading experiences they have had with their children. A slide-tape presentation about parents sharing books with their children could be developed to show to other parents.

Elementary and Junior High School Experiences[8]

As children progress through the first years of school, most of them are beginning to read independently to some degree. Their comprehension abilities have broadened greatly because they can read, as well as view and listen. Older students use attending to proceed to more complex comprehension tasks. Teachers can use attending experiences to prepare students to function on more advanced levels.

Teacher-Presented Activities

Teachers can strengthen comprehension abilities of students of all age levels by reading aloud to them. A period for reading aloud different types of literature needs to be part of the daily schedule no matter what the age of the students. Poetry, a picture book, and a part of a full-length book can be included within a literature period. A bibliography of newer poetry volumes is given in Appendix B. Appendix L contains a bibliography of books to read aloud to upper-elementary-grade children, and Appendix M is a list of picture books for older students. Students in the upper elementary and junior high grades enjoy ideas presented through picture books.

Media presentations. Films, filmstrips, tapes, records, and tapes of televised programs can all be used to strengthen attending abilities. (Appendix D contains a bibliography of media sources for literature.) Tapes which present dramatized versions of stories can enhance their appeal and understanding. For example, on the tape of Selden's book, *The Cricket in Times Square,* the cricket sings arias from operas. The casting for the taped version of Konigsburg's book, *From The Mixed-Up Files of Mrs. Basil E. Frankweiler,* makes the story come alive. Televised programs and movies can be used along with book versions of the same stories to involve students in attending. Comparing and contrasting the same story told through different media can be the basis of an interesting discussion.

Narrative pantomime. Students of all ages enjoy narrative pantomime. It involves pantomiming the action of the story while a leader reads or tells the story. It can be used to help children relate more closely to the ideas, characters, and progression of the plot. This technique is especially valuable for students who have difficulty concentrating or have short attention spans. (Appendix G contains a list of books that can be used for narrative pantomime.)

Stories and poems composed by students. Students enjoy listening to and reading materials written by themselves and their classmates. An individual student's writing can be made into a book. (Appendix N gives simple directions for making a book.) Collections of stories and poems composed by students can also be bound into books. Some librarians will accept these bound compositions and enter cards for them in the card catalog. Having an entry in the catalog can be exciting for children.

Independent Learning Centers

Centers can be utilized to extend attending experiences for older students. These youngsters need many opportunities to view, listen, and read in order to gain fluency and develop more advanced comprehension abilities. Alternative ways of attending need to be offered to students. In the centers students should be given choices, in as many cases as possible, to view, listen, or read. No student should be thwarted in receiving learning experiences because he or she does not read. (Appendix I has suggestions for independent learning centers.)

Suggestions for language activities in learning centers are as follows:

I. Centers with books to view, listen to, and read
    A. Books with no text or minimal text are available for older students. (A list of these books can be found in Appendix J.)
    B. Picture books illustrating a certain art medium, such as prints, can be used for a center. Blair Lent's article on cardboard cuts and printing, which appears in the *Horn Book,* could be developed into a center with his books and materials for students to try cardboard printing.[9] (Appendix O contains a list of picture books which illustrate art media.)
    C. Picture books and accompanying tapes, prepared by teachers, make popular centers. Fifth-and sixth-grade teachers report that this is a favorite center for their students. (Appendix M contains a bibliography of picture books for older students.) If a tape of part of a book is presented, students are often encouraged to read the rest of the book. Books such as *Soup,* by Robert Newton Peck, and *Homer Price,* by Robert McCloskey, lend themselves to one-chapter presentations.

Centers with picture books offer attending experiences for older children.

    D. Other media (films, filmstrips, tapes, records, and tapes of televised programs) can be used to present literature experiences in centers. (Appendix D gives sources of literature presented through other media.)

    E. Collections of books can be used to expand students' knowledge of a particular theme or type of literature.

        1. Centers can focus on poetry for a particular season, holiday, or concept. Children can be asked to contribute to these collections.

        2. Books representing a certain type of literature, such as science fiction or fables, can make up a center.

        3. Centers containing information about an author and the author's books can be interesting. Letters from the author, information from the author's publishing company, and taped interviews with the author can be used.

        4. A concept from any area of the curriculum could be developed into a center. Different genre (poetry, folk literature, fanciful and realistic stories, and factual materials) could be used to develop a concept. (Appendix P contains a bibliography of library references to assist teachers in finding different types of literature on particular concepts.)

        5. Factual books and biographies which deal with topics in which children are keenly interested may be the basis of a center.[10] Examples of such topics are sharks, minibikes, hot-air ballooning, hang gliding, skateboarding, jewelry making, stamp collecting, origami, guitar playing, and wrestling. Individuals of special interest to children might be O. J. Simpson, Helen Keller, and Martin Luther King.

        6. Books with a high interest level and a low reading level can give needed practice to students who are slow in acquiring reading power. Teachers need to evaluate the content of these books critically in terms of interest level. (Appendix K gives sources for books of this type.)

 II. Centers with dolls and puppets to accompany books and other media.

    Pippi Longstockings and Winnie the Pooh are just two of the many characters which are popular with children. Older students may want to make dolls and puppets to enhance listening and reading centers.

III. Center for bookmaking

    Appendix N contains directions for bookmaking.

Student-Assisted Activities

Older students can benefit from working with their peers on comprehension activities. A youngster may be paired with an older or more capable student or with another student who has a common interest. Suggestions for having older students assist with very young children are given in the section entitled "Beginning Experiences in School," subsection "Student-Assisted Activities."

Parent-Assisted Activities

Parents can make an important contribution to their children's interest in literature and language, their habits of attending to literature and language situations, and their appreciation of fine literature and well-developed language abilities. Frequently a youngster's approach to attending to literature and language is related closely to his or her parents' strategies of attending. When children in grade three or above are lagging behind in reading growth, the cause can often be attributed to the fact that these children come from non-reading homes. No newspapers and other reading materials are present; the children are not regularly taken to the library; and there are no quiet times for reading and no safe places to keep books.

Notes

1. Kenneth S. Goodman, "Acquiring Literacy Is Natural: Who Skilled Cock Robin?" *Theory into Practice,* XVI (December, 1977), 312.
2. John Burningham, *Would You Rather . . .* (New York: Thomas Y. Crowell, 1978), unpaged.
3. Alvin Tresselt, *What Did You Leave Behind?* illus. Roger Duvoisin (New York: Lothrop, Lee, and Shephard, 1978), unpaged.
4. Ruth Beall Heinig and Lyda Stillwell, *Creative Dramatics for the Classroom Teacher* (Englewood Cliffs, N.J.: Prentice-Hall, 1974).
5. Roach Van Allen, *Experiences in Communication* (Boston: Houghton Mifflin Company, 1976).
6. Marlys Priebe, Roosevelt School in Waterloo, related this experience.
7. Annabeth Gish, a student at Price Laboratory School in Cedar Falls, related this experience.
8. Many of the ideas presented in this section are more fully developed in the section entitled "Beginning Experiences in School."
9. Blair Lent, "The Artist at Work," *Horn Book,* XLI (August, 1965) 408–12.
10. A fourth-grade teacher contacted the author about a group of her students who were reading at approximately third-grade level and were uninterested in reading. Because of their lack of attention to books and story sessions, the librarian would not allow them to use the library. The author suggested that the teacher stock a center with books of high interest to the children, particularly books with many illustrations. After the children had examined the books, the teacher was advised to allow time for each student to share one interesting thing about a book with her and the other children, either by telling about the book or by reading a few pages and showing accompanying illustrations. Parts that a child could not read could be read aloud by the teacher. The teacher reported that her children spent much time each day in the center and enjoyed sharing these books. This experience led to the development of a hobby show, which was subsequently displayed in the hallway for the entire school.

Bibliography

Allen, Roach Van. *Language Experiences in Communication.* Boston: Houghton Mifflin Company, 1976.

Bailey, Carolyn Sherwin. *The Little Rabbit Who Wanted Red Wings,* illus. Dorothy Grider. New York: Platt and Munk, 1931.

Burningham, John. *Mr. Gumpy's Outing.* New York: Holt, Rinehart and Winston, 1971.

———— . *Would You Rather . . .* New York: Thomas Y. Crowell, 1978.

Emberley, Barbara. *Drummer Hoff,* illus. Ed Emberley. Englewood Cliffs, N.J.: Prentice-Hall, 1967.

Fisher, Aileen. *In the Middle of the Night,* illus. Adrienne Adams. New York: Thomas Y. Crowell, 1965.

Freeman, Don. *Dandelion*. New York: Viking Press, 1964.

Goodman, Kenneth S. "Acquiring Literacy Is Natural: Who Skilled Cock Robin?" *Theory into Practice,* XVI (December, 1977), 312–24.

Heinig, Ruth Beall, and Lyda Stillwell. *Creative Dramatics for the Classroom Teacher*. Englewood Cliffs, N.J.: Prentice-Hall, 1974.

Hogrogian, Nonny. *One Fine Day*. New York: Collier Books, 1971.

Horwitz, Elinor Lander. *When the Sky Is Like Lace,* illus. Barbara Cooney. Philadelphia: J. B. Lippincott Company, 1975.

Konigsburg, E. L. *From the Mixed-Up Files of Mrs. Basil E. Frankweiler*. New York: Atheneum, 1969.

———. *From the Mixed-Up Files of Mrs. Basil E. Frankweiler*. Tape. New York: Newbery Award Records.

Lent, Blair. "The Artist at Work." *Horn Book,* XLI (August, 1965), 408–12.

Lobel, Arnold. *Frog and Toad Are Friends*. New York: Harper and Row, 1970.

———. *Frog and Toad Together*. New York: Harper and Row, 1972.

McCloskey, Robert. *Blueberries for Sal*. New York: Viking Press, 1948.

———. *Homer Price*. New York: Viking Press, 1943.

———. *Make Way for Ducklings*. New York: Viking Press, 1941.

———. *Time of Wonder*. New York: Viking Press, 1957.

———. *Lively Art of Picture Books,* Part II. Film. Weston, Conn.: Weston Woods Studio, 1964.

McDermott, Gerald. *Anansi the Spider*. New York: Holt, Rinehart and Winston, 1972.

———. *Anansi the Spider*. Film. Texture Film, 1977.

Montresor, Beni. *Bedtime*. New York: Harper and Row, 1978.

Nixon, Joan Lowery. *The Alligator Under the Bed,* illus. Jan Hughes. New York: G. P. Putnam's Sons, 1974.

Peck, Robert Newton. *Soup*. New York: Alfred A. Knopf, 1974.

Ryan, Cheli Duran. *Hildilid's Night,* illus. Arnold Lobel. New York: Macmillan Publishing Company, 1971.

Selden, George. *The Cricket in Times Square*. New York: Farrar, Straus and Giroux, 1960.

———. *The Cricket in Times Square*. Tape. New York: Newbery Award Records.

Tresselt, Alvin. *What Did You Leave Behind?* illus. Roger Duvoisin. New York: Lothrop, Lee, and Shephard, 1978.

Williams, Barbara. *Albert's Toothache*. New York: E. P. Dutton, 1974.

Yolen, Jane. *No Bath Tonight,* illus. Nancy Winslow Parker. New York: Thomas Y. Crowell, 1978.

Literal Understanding

Literal understanding involves comprehending and responding to ideas that are presented explicitly. Most students in kindergarten through grade eight can understand ideas expressed explicitly if they have a sufficient background of experiences.

Cognitive and Affective Tasks

Representatiave cognitive and affective behaviors of literal understanding are as follows:

I. Cognitive tasks
   A. Notes elements, such as
      1. Sequence of ideas
      2. Direct statements of characters and setting
      3. Description of characters and statements of idea development
      4. Supporting details of main idea or theme
      5. Point of view of storyteller
      6. Imagery
      7. Sound elements of language
   B. Notes features or parts of specific types of stories, such as humorous stories and fairy tales
   C. Recognizes organizational patterns
II. Affective tasks
   A. Responds emotionally to elements and features in light of personal experiences
   B. Empathizes with certain characters and events
   C. Relates work to personal experiences and knowledge of the world
   D. Examines personal feelings evoked by a work
   E. Listens to the others' responses to a work

Because of the nature of literature, literal understanding can involve cognitive and affective responses simultaneously. For example, as young children follow the sequence of events in the picture book *Albert's Toothache,* by Williams, they seem to empathize with the character, Albert, because they too may have experienced tooth problems. Children frequently respond with surprise and appear pleased and satisfied with the outcome of the story. After an upper-elementary teacher finished reading Gipson's *Old Yeller* to her class, a boy told her with a shaky voice that he did not like the ending of the story. To alleviate his grief for Old Yeller, the teacher suggested that he read the sequel, *Savage Sam.* As he read that story, he kept remarking enthusiastically to his teacher that the pup, Savage Sam, was just like Old Yeller.

These children are enjoying the many fascinating details in the illustrations of *Anna's Journey,* a picture book without words.

As the boy in this example demonstrates, children often respond emotionally to literature. These responses need to be capitalized on to improve literal comprehension. Thomas, a first-grader, spent much of his out-of-school time participating in athletic activities and watching sports events with his father. This black boy identified closely with well-known black athletes. His mother supported this interest and at the same time promoted an interest in reading and composition by taking him to the public library each week and helping him select simple biographies of black athletes. She read them to him and then wrote down the stories as he retold them to her. She stapled the pages of Thomas' stories together to make books. Thomas brought these books to school, and his teacher read them to the class.

After a sixth-grade teacher read the book *Christmas in Iowa,* by Andrews, she encouraged her students to think about memorable Christmases they had had in their family and to ask the older members of their family about their experiences with Christmas. One student related that her grandmother, who had grown up in Amana, had told her that in the early days, the people did not cut trees to decorate for Christmas but decorated brooms instead. The stories these sixth graders shared in school were written up and compiled into a book.[1]

Incorporating the interests of students into learning experiences at school can provide motivation to read. Interests can propel students to read more difficult materials and to sustain their involvement in reading much longer than would be thought possible. A language arts teacher in a junior high school found that many of the boys in her classes were not progressing commensurate with their abilities. Many of these boys were from rural families and dreamed of the day when they would farm. With the help of the librarian and the students, the teacher developed a reading center containing agribusiness journals, bulletins from the Extension Service, and magazines such as *Popular Mechanics.* Not only did the boys start to read avidly but they began to use higher comprehension tasks. As a result of their reading, they listed current issues in agribusiness, and some of the boys read in depth on these issues.

Finding out what children are interested in and then giving them opportunities to respond to these interests seems to be a more effective teaching strategy than questioning them about who, what, where, and when after a viewing, listening, or reading experience. It is extremely important for teachers to observe closely the responses of children in order to find topics and ideas that spark their curiosity. Not only can interest lead to the strengthening of comprehension abilities but it may lead to a pastime in adult life.

Experiences with literal understanding tasks can be used to build a background for higher intellectual and affective responses. In discussing Wier's *The Loner,* students (usually in grades five to eight) can be asked to recall the sequence of ideas. These ideas can be charted as shown in Appendix Q. If students are capable of engaging in interpretation tasks, the chart can be used to infer character development and to consider the relationship of the character development and the theme of the story. Such an exercise calling for the use of higher comprehension abilities can provide a real challenge for gifted children.

Experiences with Literal Understanding[2]

Language programs need to provide many opportunities for students to respond to the explicit ideas and related emotional qualities encountered in different forms of comprehension (viewing, listening, and reading). These experiences can be presented by teachers directly or in independent learning centers.

In selecting stories and poems to read aloud or to present in independent learning centers, teachers should consider those suitable for interpretation and evaluation. Appropriate selections will help students understand elements and features and respond to emotional qualities inherent in stories and poems. When teachers understand the potential of literature experiences for higher levels of comprehension, they are more prepared to assist children in moving beyond literal understanding tasks.

Teacher-Presented Activities

Teachers can extend students' experiences with the cognitive and affective aspects of literal understanding by reading aloud to them and then providing time to discuss the ideas found in the selections. (In Chapter I, the benefits of providing for discussions are developed more fully.)

Teachers can collect stories and poems that are related to each other in terms of characters, images, events, concepts, personal-social functions, and movement of language. For example, the picture book *The Red Balloon,* by Lamorisse, can be used with the poem

"Balloon!" by Thurman. Both the picture book *Guess Who My Favorite Person Is,* by Baylor, and the poem "This Man Talked About You," by Ciardi, present the idea of friendship and can be used with a wide age range. Sisters are troublesome in the picture book *A Baby Sister for Frances,* by Hoban, and the poems "For Sale," by Silverstein, and "Spoiled Sister Song," by Livingston. Yet in Grimes' poem, a sister is special "Cause she believes in me." The marching rhythm in the picture book *Drummer Hoff,* by Emberley, and the Mother Goose poem "The Grand Old Duke of York" are similar. Comparing and contrasting elements and generalizing about ideas from different literature selections are interpretation tasks suitable for students who can cope with more advanced thinking experiences.

Teachers can also provide experiences with literal understanding through media presentations, flannelboard stories, dramatization and narrative pantomime, puppets, and story and poetry composition.

Media presentations. Different types of media presentations (films, filmstrips, records, tapes, and televised programs) can offer alternatives to reading and different perspectives of characters, events, and ideas. Appendix D contains a list of sources of literature experiences presented through media. Many fine works of literature have been adapted for media presentations.

Flannelboard stories. The sequence of ideas and the patterns of plot in stories can be portrayed visually through flannelboard stories. Examples of plot organizations that can be presented through flannelboard stories are (1) patterns of three *(The Three Bill Goats Gruff,* Berson's *Joseph and the Snake);* (2) cumulative tales (Kruskin's *A Boy Had a Mother Who Bought Him a Hat,* Hogrogian's *One Fine Day*); (3) full circle (Brown's *Once a Mouse,* Hoffman's *Hans in Luck;* and (4) cause and effect (Barton's *Buzz Buzz Buzz*). Other examples of books with interesting plot structures suitable for flannelboards are given in Appendix C, Literature, Language and Thought.

Dramatizations and narrative pantomime. For students of all ages, drama experiences can expand literal understanding. Dramatizations offer children opportunities to explore the ideas and events of stories and the feelings and motives of characters. After Galdone's version of *The Three Bears* was published, a third-grade teacher presented it to her class, along with the idea that many folk tales were now being published individually in picture books. After she had read the story, she showed two pictures of Goldilocks from the book and asked the class what they thought of her. A boy replied that she was a brat. Following the discussion, a small group of children in the class developed a dramatization of the story in which Goldilocks was portrayed as frightened and helpless—quite different from Galdone's character. Through dramatization, students can manipulate the elements of stories and develop their own points of view.

Flannelboard stories can be used to recall sequences of ideas.

Narrative pantomime experiences allow children to recall elements of a story such as characters and idea development and to manipulate these ideas and feelings through body movements. Sources of stories suitable for use with narrative pantomime are given in Appendix G.

Puppetry. Experiences with puppetry can assist students to comprehend elements and features of stories. Through puppetry, students can respond to the emotional elements of stories and can examine their personal feelings and those of others evoked by the work. Simple folk tales are highly adaptable for students of all ages to use in initial experiences with puppetry. The characters and development of ideas are presented simply and clearly. Good overcomes evil, usually because of the ingenuity of one of the characters. Plot sequences are clearly organized. Examples are patterns of three, full circle, and cause and effect. Appendix C, Literature, Language and Thought, contains examples of stories with different plot organizations.

The boy at the left interviewed a well-known athlete and wrote an article about him for the school newspaper. After having listened to the taped interview, the boy and his friends are reading the article.

Stories and poems composed by students. By composing and reading their own stories and poems and those of others, students can expand their understanding of elements, features, and organizational patterns. Emotional responses can also be shared and examined. If students experience the process of developing interesting characters and portraying a clear sequence of ideas, their understanding of the communication process is deepened.

Independent Learning Centers

Teachers can use learning centers to extend students' involvement in literal comprehension tasks. The chapter on attention has suggestions for the use of learning centers and comments about specific types of centers.

Suggestions for using learning centers to strengthen literal understanding abilities are as follows:

I. Viewing and reading centers
   A. A collection of picture books and full-length books can be organized around interesting characters from realistic fiction, folk literature such as Nordic tales, and personified animal stories. Students can be asked to contribute to the center. Dolls

and puppets representing characters in books can also be featured. Examples for young children are Frances, from Hoban's Frances books; Max and the wild things, from Sendak's *Where the Wild Things Are;* Little Bear, from Minarik's Little Bear books; the mouse, Anatole, from Titus' Anatole books; Harry, the dog, from Zion's Harry the Dirty Dog books; and Corduroy, the bear, from Freeman's book of the same title. Examples interesting to older children are the Pooh characters; Laura Ingalls' doll, Charlotte; Dandelion, from Freeman's book of the same title; Pippi Longstockings; and folk figures, such as a troll, a tomten from Lindren's *The Tomten,* and a bunyip from Wagner's *The Bunyip of Berkeley's Creek.* Sources of picture books are Appendix A, Books for Young Children; Appendix R, Literature for Children in Grades Two and Three; and Appendix M, Picture Books for Older Children.

B. A collection of books can be organized around a concept. One second-grade room had a center on bears, and the children brought their stuffed bears to place in the center. The concept can be presented through different kinds of books, such as factual, various types of fiction, and poetry.

C. A collection of poems representing different forms and points of view can develop a concept. Examples of forms that can be included are concrete poetry, cinquain, haiku, and diamante. Appendix H presents many different forms of poetry. In presenting a concept, for example, wind, the teacher could include poems with different points of view, such as poems about wind, poems with the wind speaking, and those having someone or something speaking to the wind.

D. Development of a similar idea can provide the unifying theme of a collection of stories and poems. For example, difficulty with a baby sibling entering into the family may be of concern to young children. Older students may enjoy reading and sharing books about boys and girls who are working toward a goal. In Paterson's *The Great Gilly Hopkins,* Gilly is trying to find her mother. Bert, in Edmond's *Bert Breen's Barn,* is struggling to move a barn. Jenny, in Bell's *Jenny's Corner,* is trying to protect wild animals in her region from hunters. In *Words by Heart,* by Sebestyen, Lena is working to win the memory verse contest. A center might be developed around different experiences with night. For many children, night can be frightening and filled with unexplainable sensory experiences. In the picture book *When the Sky Is Like Lace,* by Horwitz, night is portrayed as wonderfully exciting and magical. Night also is viewed positively in Fisher's *In the Middle of the Night.* A young girl asks to be allowed to stay up all night for her birthday. With her father, she explores the wonders of night. In both books, the mood of positive encounters with night is accentuated by the stories being told in verse. The stories have a songlike quality. *Hildilid's Night,* by Ryan, takes a humorous look at night. Hildilid attempts to get rid of the night but only succeeds in wearing herself out. She goes to bed as the sun is coming up.

After these eighth graders had studied monsters and other large, imaginary characters, they composed stories for a booklet and drew pictures.

E. A center can be formed from a collection of stories and poems that explicitly present a specific literary element, such as repetition and refrain, imagery, patterns of three, and cumulative plot. Examples of books that contain different elements can be found in Appendix C, Literature, Language and Thought. Picture books can assist children in noting different elements and features in stories and poems. The content is brief, and the illustrations often portray in a concrete way the characters, events, plot sequence, and organization of the story. In the fable, *Once a Mouse,* by Brown, the illustrations support the text in portraying a full circle plot. In *A Boy Had a Mother Who Bought Him a Hat,* by Kuskin, and *The Judge,* by Zemach, the accumulation of ideas in the respective plots is clearly shown in both the text and the illustrations.

F. Groups of picture books and full-length books representing specific types of stories, such as humorous stories or personified animal stories, can make up a center. This type of collection can help students to recognize and understand the features associated with different types of stories and poems.

II. Viewing and listening centers

Different types of media can be used to present literature selections in centers. Appendix D gives sources of media adaptations of literature selections.

III. Viewing, listening, and reading centers
  A. Tapes or records of the text of a book (commercially prepared or teacher-made) can be used either alone or with the accompanying book in the center. The suggestions in the section on viewing and reading in this chapter can be used with tapes and records.
  B. Poetry experiences are enhanced if the poems are presented orally. To further literal understanding of specific elements, centers can focus on the different sensory aspects of imagery (sight, sound, touch, taste, and smell) or the various sound elements in poetry (rhyme, rhythm, and repetition).
  C. With primary-age children, flannelboard pieces can be used to accompany books, tapes, and records or to retell the story after it is read or listened to. Flannelboard experiences help to extend children's understanding of the sequence of ideas and the organizational plan of stories (patterns of three, full circle, and cumulative). Appendix F contains a list of books that make interesting flannelboard stories.
  D. Similar versions of a folk tale found in different parts of the world can be presented in an independent center and then discussed. The various aspects of the different versions can be compared and contrasted. For example, illustrated versions of Cinderella could be used, such as Perrault's French version, translated and illustrated by Marcia Brown; Grimm's German version, illustrated by Svend Otto S.; and a Vietnamese version, *In the Land of Small,* told by Dang Manh Kha to Ann Nolan Clark and illustrated by Tony Chen.

   A group of third graders compared these three versions of Rumpelstiltskin: a Cornish version, *Duffy and the Devil,* retold by Zemach; an English version, *Tom Tit Tot,* retold by Ness; and a Geman version, found in Arbuthnot's collection, *Time for Poetry.* (This activity also is appropriate for students in the upper elementary and junior high school years.) These aspects of the stories were compared and contrasted:

      What the girls were like
      Who their masters were
      How they came to their masters and how they got work they could not do
      Who offered to help them do their work
      What the payment was for the work
      How long did they have to guess the name of the evil one
      How the name of the evil creature was discovered
      What the name of the creature was
      What the evil creature's response was when his name was revealed
      What the future will be for the girls (a topic for interpretation)

  E. Through dioramas, models, puppets, and murals, students can manipulate literal ideas encountered in literature.
    1. A scene from a story can be developed into a diorama. A box can house the characters, props, and scenery. The characters can be made of clay, cardboard, cornhusks, or other materials.

2. Clay models of fanciful characters from books and poems are interesting to make. Examples are the characters from Wagner's *The Bunyip of Berkeley's Creek,* Tolkien's *The Hobbit,* de Larrabeiti's *The Borribles,* and Prelutsky's book of poems, *The Snopp on the Sidewalk.* Older students enjoy making models of inanimate objects, such as ships and robots.

3. Puppets representing characters can be developed easily and quickly from scrap materials. Books such as Alkema's *Puppet-Making* and Gates' *Glove, Mitten, and Sock Puppets* give directions for making many kinds of simple puppets. Shadow puppets can also be made.

4. Murals can be developed which depict parts of a book. After the mural is planned, its parts can be assigned to different groups of youngsters.

IV. Bookmaking center

The bookmaking center is one of the most popular learning centers. It seems to supply motivation to read and compose. Simple bookbinding directions, suitabale for young children, are given in Chapter II, in the section entitled "Beginning Experiences in School." Directions for older students are given in Appendix N.

Notes

1. Barbara Scott, Squaw Creek Elementary School, Cedar Rapids Community Schools, shared this experience.
2. Many of the activities in this section are also discussed in Chapter II, Attention, and in some cases they are developed more thoroughly in that chapter.

Bibliography

Alkema, Chester Jay. *Puppet-Making.* New York: Sterling Publishing Company, 1971.

Andrews, Clarence, ed. *Christmas in Iowa.* Iowa City, Ia: Midwest Heritage Publishing Company, 1979.

Arbuthnot, May Hill, and Shelton L. Root, Jr. (compil.). *Time for Poetry.* 3rd ed. Chicago: Scott, Foresman and Company, 1970.

Arbuthnot, May Hill and Mark Taylor (compil.). *Time for Old Magic.* Chicago: Scott, Foresman and Company, 1969.

Barton, Byron. *Buzz Buzz Buzz.* New York: Macmillan Publishing Company, 1973.

Baylor, Byrd. *Guess Who My Favorite Person Is,* illus. Robert Andrew Parker. New York: Charles Scribner's Sons, 1977.

————— . *The Other Way To Listen,* illus. Peter Parnall. New York: Charles Scribner's Sons, 1978.

Bell, Frederic. *Jenny's Corner.* New York: Random House, 1974.

Berson, Joseph. *Joseph and the Snake.* New York: Macmillan Publishing Company, 1979.

Brown, Marcia. *Cinderella.* New York: Charles Scribner's Sons, 1954.

————— . *Once a Mouse.* New York: Charles Scribner's Sons, 1961.

Ciardi, John. *I Met a Man.* Boston: Houghton Mifflin Company, 1961.

Clark, Ann Nolan. *In the Land of Small Dragon,* illus. Tony Chen. New York: Viking Press, 1979.

de Larrabeiti, Michael. *The Borribles.* New York: Macmillan Publishing Company, 1976.

Edmonds, Walter. *Bert Breen's Barn.* Boston: Little, Brown and Company, 1975.

Emberley, Barbara. *Drummer Hoff,* illus. Ed Emberley. Englewood Cliffs, N.J.: Prentice-Hall, 1967.

Fisher, Aileen. *In the Middle of the Night,* illus. Adrienne Adams. New York: Thomas Y. Crowell Company, 1965.

Freeman, Don. *Corduroy.* New York: Viking Press, 1968.

Galdone, Paul. *The Three Bears.* New York: Seabury Press, 1972.

Gates, Frieda. *Glove, Mitten, and Sock Puppets.* New York: Walker and Company, 1978.

Gipson, Fred. *Old Yeller.* New York: Harper and Row, 1956.

———— . *Savage Sam.* New York: Harper and Row, 1962.

Grimes, Nikki. *Something on My Mind,* illus. Tom Feelings. New York: Dial Press, 1972.

Grimm. *Cinderella,* illus. Svend Otto S. New York: Larousse and Company, 1978.

Hoban, Russell. *A Baby Sister for Frances,* illus. Lillian Hoban. New York: Harper and Row, 1964.

Hoffman, Felix. *Hans in Luck.* New York: Atheneum, 1975.

Hogrogian, Nonny. *One Fine Day.* New York: Collier Books, 1971.

Horwitz, Elinor Lander. *When the Sky Is Like Lace,* illus. Barbara Cooney. Philadelphia: J. B. Lippincott Company, 1975.

Kuskin, Karla. *A Boy Had a Mother Who Bought Him a Hat.* Boston: Houghton Mifflin Company, 1976.

Lamorisse, Albert. *The Red Balloon.* Garden City, N.Y.: Doubleday and Company, 1956.

Lindren, Astrid. *The Tomten,* illus. Harald Wiberg. New York: Coward-McCann, 1961.

Livingston, Myra Cohn. *4-Way Stop.* New York: Atheneum, 1976.

Minarik, Else Holmelund. *Father Bear Comes Home,* illus. Maurice Sendak. New York: Harper and Row, 1959.

———— . *A Kiss for Little Bear,* illus. Maurice Sendak. New York: Harper and Row, 1968.

———— . *Little Bear,* illus. Maurice Sendak. New York: Harper and Row, 1975.

———— . *Little Bear's Friend,* illus. Maurice Sendak. New York: Harper and Row, 1960.

———— . *Little Bear's Visit,* illus. Maurice Sendak. New York: Harper and Row, 1961.

Mother Goose. "The Grand Old Duke of York." *Time for Poetry,* compil. May Hill Arbuthnot and Shelton L. Root, Jr. 3rd ed. Chicago: Scott Foresman Company, 1968.

Ness, Evaline. *Tom Tit Tot.* New York: Charles Scribner's Sons, 1965.

Paterson, Katherine. *The Great Gilly Hopkins.* New York: Thomas Y. Crowell Company, 1978.

Prelutsky, Jack. *The Snopp on the Sidewalk,* illus. Byron Barton. New York: William Morrow and Company, 1977.

Ryan, Cheli Duran. *Hildilid's Night,* illus. Arnold Lobel. New York: Macmillan Publishing Company, 1971.

Sebestyen, Ouida. *Words by Heart.* Boston: Little, Brown and Company, 1979.

Sendak, Maurice. *Where the Wild Things Are.* New York: Harper and Row, 1963.

Silverstein, Shel. "For Sale." *Oh That's Ridiculous!* compil. William Cole and illus. Tomi Ungerer. New York: Viking Press, 1972.

Thurman, Judith. *Flashlight.* New York: Atheneum, 1976.

Titus, Eve. *Anatole,* illus. Paul Galdone. New York: Lothrop, Lee, and Shephard, 1956.

Tolkien, J. R. R. *The Hobbit.* Boston: Houghton Mifflin Company, 1938.

Wagner, Jenny. *The Bunyip of Berkeley's Creek,* illus. Ron Brooks. Scarsdale, N.Y.: Bradbury Press, 1973.

Wier, Ester. *The Loner.* New York: David McKay Company, 1963.

Williams, Barbara. *Albert's Toothache.* New York: E. P. Dutton and Company, 1974.

Zemach, Harve and Margot. *Duffy and the Devil.* New York: Farrar, Straus and Giroux, 1973.

———— . *The Judge,* illus. Margot Zemach. New York: Farrar, Straus and Giroux, 1969.

Zion, Gene. *Harry, the Dirty Dog,* illus. Margaret Bloy Graham. New York: Harper and Row, 1956.

Interpretation

On the interpretation level, children manipulate ideas and bring their imagination and knowledge of the world into the comprehension process. They use inductive and deductive reasoning. On this level, children are able to see relationships among ideas expressed explicitly and to understand ideas expressed implicitly. Interpretation, as with attention and literal understanding, involves cognitive and affective tasks.

For students who have sufficient intellectual and social-emotional development and background of experiences, interpretation tasks offer a greater understanding and appreciation of language and literature. A part of the beauty of Yolen's picture book *The Seeing Stick* is the relationship of the illustrations and the idea development. Many of Julia Cunningham's books seem like story puzzles because they have more than one layer of meaning.

Not only does involvement in interpretation tasks allow for a deeper understanding of viewing, listening, and reading experiences, but it may lead to the rediscovery of various works and different types of literature. Young children find the story and illustrations of Lionni's *Frederick* appealing, but older students gain further appreciation of the fable through understanding its theme. Young children enjoy folk tales but rediscover this genre when they are able to respond with more developed abilities and a wider background of experiences. Then folk tales not only can be enjoyed for their interesting characters, idea development, and plot structures, but different versions can be compared and contrasted and generalizations can be made about common themes and motifs.

Interpretation tasks can pose a challenge for students, but sometimes these tasks are omitted because teachers fear that they will be seen as too analytical of the material. This problem can be eliminated if the teacher carefully analyzes a work for its uniqueness as a piece of literature, rather than discussing it paragraph by paragraph or presenting every element and relationship in the work. The emphasis needs to be on the whole work rather than on parts and elements.

Interpretation tasks should flow naturally from attending and literal understanding experiences. They should not be sessions in which students are frustrated by trying to find an author's hidden meaning or by trying to understand a relationship that the teacher finds in a work. Experiences with viewing, listening, and reading need to be planned in a way that allows interpretation to take place if students have the ability, background of experiences, and motivation to operate on that level. Carefully selected questions involving literal comprehension can serve as a basis for students to move to more advanced tasks of comprehension.

As children start to develop logical thought processes, they can begin to engage in interpretative tasks. Usually by the time students are seven or eight years of age, they are capable of more flexible and analytical thinking. They are able to follow logically a sequence of ideas, to perceive the elements and features in a work or an event, to move from one idea to another, to think about ideas through language without relying on bodily movements, to

Guided discussion of selected picture books can assist children in becoming involved in interpretation tasks.

be less self-oriented in approaching tasks, and to make generalizations about ideas and events. Children from approximately seven or eight to eleven or twelve years of age are able to manipulate language in situations closely related to their experiences. For example, many ten-year-olds will understand the metaphor associating robots with utility lines in Myra Cohn Livingston's poem, "Power Lines," because they have had concrete experiences with these concepts. The title of Belting's book, *Whirlwind Is a Ghost Dancing,* is a metaphor which may be more distant from children's experiences and therefore more difficult to understand.

Many students moving toward the end of the elementary years and into the junior high school years are able to perform more advanced comprehension tasks. They can deal with ideas in the abstract and in the past and future and can coordinate ideas rather than dealing with them in isolation. With these capabilities and a good background of experiences with language and literature, students can take part in a wide range of sophisticated comprehension tasks. For example, they can generalize about a common theme contained in several books. They can examine stories and poems for abstractions, symbols, or different levels of interpretation. They can consider the contributions of different types of literature to the understanding of an idea or a concept. Students can begin to manipulate ideas contrary to fact by interjecting certain events and characters in a situation and speculating on the outcome, by substituting another value system for that of characters and cultures in the past and making conjectures on the results, or by analyzing the options of a contemporary society and hypothesizing about the future.

Because the cognitive and affective tasks of interpretation are complicated, they are discussed in separate sections along with suggested school experiences. Many of these experiences can be presented by the teacher or adapted for independent learning centers. Activities to help develop interpretation abilities are discussed in Chapter II, Attention, and Chapter III, Literal Understanding. Lists of other useful materials and activities are contained in the appendices.

Cognitive Tasks and School Experiences

In the effort to challenge students and to develop their thinking abilities and understanding of literature, the relationship of the comprehension tasks to each other and to the whole work must not be overlooked. The focus in a school experience needs to be on the work, whether a viewing, listening, or reading experience, and the inherent tasks and their relationships in a work. In this section, the development of representative cognitive tasks of interpretation will be discussed as well as representative relationships among the tasks.

Representative cognitive tasks are as follows:

A. Understands elements such as
    1. Sequence of ideas
    2. Character delineation
    3. Character and idea development
    4. Supporting details of a main idea or theme
    5. Plot devices
    6. Point of view of storyteller
    7. Mood
    8. Imagery
    9. Figurative language
    10. Sound elements of language
    11. Style
B. Recognizes characteristics of different types of literature.
C. Relates elements to one another
    1. Relates characters and actions to plot
    2. Predicts outcomes and forms conclusions
    3. Understands literary elements as clues to meaning
    4. Relates ideas to each other
    5. Recognizes organizational patterns
D. Considers elements and parts as they relate to the meaning of the whole work
E. Detects relationships between characters as reflections of meaning
F. Understands the contributions of different types of literature to the understanding of an idea or a concept
G. Sees different levels of meaning in a work
H. Recognizes the intention of an author

Understands Elements

Studying selected elements may clarify the meaning of a work. The nature of individual elements must be understood before the relationships between and among these elements can be grasped.

Sequence of ideas. Occasionally the author does not present the sequence of ideas in an explicit manner. To understand the story or poem, students must conjecture. In Sperry's *Call It Courage,* it is not clear whether Mafatu collapses of exhaustion or dies as he returns home. At the end of O'Brien's *Mrs. Frisby and the Rats of NIMH,* the fate of the animals in the new valley is not told. Writing a sequel would be an interesting experience for older students.

Organizational patterns such as flashbacks (Byars' *The House of Wings* and Hunter's *The Third Eye*) and cumulative plots ("The Woman and Her Pig" in Arbuthnot's *Time for Old Magic* and Zemach's *It Could Always Be Worse*) can be examined for their effect on the flow of ideas in a story and on the audience.

In some stories, the sequence of ideas builds to a climax, and then the problem or conflict is resolved. Sperry's *Call It Courage* includes a series of minor climaxes followed by a final climax of great intensity.

Character delineation. Inferences can be made about character traits on the basis of explicit clues. One interesting exercise for students would be to study the characters in Tom Sawyer and match their traits to the characteristics of astrological signs.[1]

As students have experiences with character delineation in literature, they can begin to generalize about the qualities of characters and understand their degree of wholeness and humanness. In folk literature, the goodness and evil of characters are presented clearly. This quality makes the characterizations in folk tales timeless. Students can begin to see that realistic fiction reflects society's view of individuality and human rights. Older students can have an interesting experience tracing the change in attitudes toward minorities and the corresponding change in their characterization in movies and books. In contemporary realistic fiction, not only is a wider range of characters portrayed, but the role of characters is broader, more varied, and therefore less stereotyped. For example, mothers are now portrayed in many different ways, as people with strengths and weaknesses. The mother is not always gentle, long-suffering, and self-sacrificing; she may have goals for her own fulfillment. Others may assume some of her responsibilities for parenting. In Gripe's *The Night Daddy,* an adult male babysits with Julia while her mother works. Laura Ingalls Wilder's view of human beings was unique for her era because in the 1930's, she dared to let Ma make a mistake. When the neighbor girl wanted Laura's doll, Ma insisted that the unwilling Laura give up her doll, which Laura later found frozen in a water puddle.

Characters and idea development. In some works, it can be inferred that the characters gain a particular understanding of themselves, others, and the world in which they live. As a result, they develop and change. Paterson's *The Great Gilly Hopkins* is such a work. Gilly, the tough foster child, is totally absorbed in getting her way, but by the end of the story she has changed a great deal and now considers her grandmother's needs as well as her own.

Recognition of implied ideas may create further understanding and appreciation of the work. In Horwitz' *When the Sky Is Like Lace,* the idea that night is magic is implicitly developed by a description of what can happen on a bimulous night when the sky is like lace.

Supporting details. Supporting details that are implicitly stated can often provide clues to the idea development. In Freeman's *Dandelion,* no reason is explicitly given for the character Dandelion going as a dandy to Jennifer Giraffe's come-as-you-are party.

Plot devices. Older students can begin to understand the effect of different plot devices on the telling of a story. They are able to speculate on an author's motives in using a specific plot device. Repetition and refrain, pattern of three, and cumulative plot encourage anticipation and participation from the audience. Surprise endings can bring pleasure to the audience and can strengthen the author's idea development. In Yolen's picture book *The Seeing Stick,* the impact of finding out that the old man who came to teach the emperor's daughter is also blind leads to a sudden awareness of the teacher's insight into the problems of his pupil. The surprise ending in Heide's *Banana Twist,* a book for older students, can bring a humorous response and speculation about the two neighbor boys' experiences as roommates in a boys' boarding school. The surprise ending might serve as a springboard for a sequel.

In order to give more than one point of view, storytellers may simultaneously present different plots. In Burningham's *Come Away From the Water, Shirley,* the author-illustrator uses parallel plots to show two perspectives of an experience at the beach. On the righthand page, the parents warn their daughter Shirley about going near the water. Shirley, on the lefthand page, stays safely on the beach, but in her imagination she moves out to sea and has a dangerous encounter with pirates. Shector, in the picture book *Conrad's Castles,* also uses parallel plot to show fantasy and reality. The fantasy plot moves across the top of the page while the realistic plot moves along the bottom part. Conrad ascends a ladder into the air to build a castle; he uses his imagination to reach a goal. Konigsburg, in *Father's Arcane Daughter,* uses parallel plot to give perspective to the childhood experiences of two persons. One plot involves events in their childhood; the other is a discussion and interpretation of these events by the same characters as adults.

Flashbacks can be used to give a more meaningful perspective to the story. For example, Betsy Byars begins *The House of Wings* with a dramatic scene: an old man searching for a fleeing boy. In the flashback, that follows soon afterward, the reader learns that the boy and his parents, on their way to establish a new home in Detroit, visit the grandfather, who is a stranger to the boy. While the boy is asleep, the parents go on to Detroit, leaving the boy, who is unaware of their plans, with his grandfather. In Blos' *A Gathering of Days,* an elderly woman tells her great granddaughter about a critical time in her girlhood, prior to the Civil War. This flashback to life sixty-five years before in rural New England is a vehicle for the great grandmother to share the special understanding and relationships she gained through the events of a year and a half.

Point of view of storyteller. The point of view expressed in a story or poem can affect the idea development. Poems which are about a common idea or event but have different points of view could be compared and contrasted, such as poems telling about the night, poems in which the night speaks, and poems in which the night is being addressed. Students might enjoy telling a common folk tale from the first-person point of view of one of the characters. For example, a student could portray Baby Bear of *The Three Bears* while recounting the story during sharing time at school.

In most folk tales, the story is slanted more favorably toward the protagonist(s) or the character(s) representing the forces of good. Students could retell the folk tale from the point of view of the antagonist, for example, the troll in *The Three Billy Goats Gruff*. The character of the wolf in *Little Red Riding Hood* could be changed from a villain to a hero, and then the story could be told from the wolf's point of view. The manipulation of the point of view of folk tales can be the basis for interesting puppet shows for older students to give to their peers.

In Von Cannon's *The Moonclock,* the story of a young woman in seventeenth century Austria is told through the correspondence of several characters, each of whom has a different point of view of the events. Many junior high students will be fascinated by the details of life in Vienna, the conflicts between people who were enlightened and those who were ruled by superstition, and the roles men and women were expected to fulfill.

Events in characters' lives can be more fully understood by presenting their different points of view. In Gripe's *Julia's House,* the effort to save a house from demolition is described from the point of view of a female child and from that of an adult male. In St. George's *The Halo Wind,* the white girl and the Indian girl look at the wagon train crossing the mountains into Oregon from different points of view. The white girl sees the journey as a part of the process of establishing a home; the Indian girl perceives it as an invasion which will lead to the eventual destruction of her people's way of life.

Presenting different points of view can give the audience a clearer picture of the relationships among the characters. In Hartling's *Oma,* common experiences are related from the point of view of an orphaned boy and from that of his elderly grandmother with whom he lives. In *The Stones,* Hickman contrasts the point of view of adults toward the elderly and the actions of boys toward an elderly man. Through role switching, the girl in Rodgers' *Freaky Friday* gains more appreciation for her mother's abilities and responsibilities as a homemaker.

Mood. Sensing the mood of stories and poems can help children comprehend ideas. A wide range of moods needs to be presented. In Myra Cohn Livingston's volume of poetry *4-Way Stop,* many different moods are presented, for example, the sadness of loosing one's dog in "For Mugs," the humor of a "Conversation with Washington" about the date of his birthday being changed, and the frustration of having someone eat all the cookies in "Revenge." In Peck's book *Soup,* most of the episodes of the friends, Soup and Robert, are hilarious, yet Peck includes a sobering chapter about sharing new possessions with a friend. The text and illustration of McCloskey's *Time of Wonder* present a range of moods: happy summer activity at the beach, the darkness of night time, the rage of the storm, and the sunny calm after the storm.

Imagery and figurative language. Imagery and figurative language can make experiences with language and literature more meaningful and vivid. In many instances, imagery and figurative language are interwoven in a work. These elements frequently are found in poems and contribute to the strength of the ideas and feelings. Through imagery, selected words present sensory experiences in a story or poem. For example, the picture book *When the Sky Is Like Lace,* by Horwitz, has many examples of imagery: "everything is strange-splendid and plum-purple," "the trees eucalyptus back and forth, forth and back, swishing and swaying, swaying and swishing," "smells like gooseberry jam," and "feels like the velvet inside a very old violin case."[2] In the picture books *Guess Who My Favorite Person Is,* by Baylor, and *What Did You Leave Behind?* by Tresselt, the authors use imagery to invite the listener or reader to have a more complete understanding of the experiences. Baylor explores in depth sensory experiences with nature in the picture book *The Other Way To Listen.*

Figurative language involves the association of one idea with another. One figure of speech, the metaphor, is an implied comparison, such as "the fog comes on little cat feet."[3] The simile, on the other hand, involves an explicit comparison, for example, "when the sky is like lace." For most children in the elementary grades, figurative language should deal with experiences with which they are familiar.

Sound elements of language. The sounds of language—rhythm, rhyme, and repetition—enrich stories and poems. Greenfield's "Rope Rhyme," in *Honey, I Love,* incorporates a jumping rhythm into a poem about jumping rope. Rhyming lines, alliteration (repetition of the beginning sounds of words), and repetition of lines and stanzas can encourage anticipation and participation. Children seem to learn poetry without any conscious effort. Alliteration can emphasize ideas. The repetition of words beginning with the soft consonant sounds such as "s" or "sh" gives a quiet, comforting feeling to a story or poem, as in Bacmeister's poem "Galoshes," in Arbuthnot's collection *Time for Poetry:* "Susie's galoshes/ Makes splishes and sploshes/ And slooshes and sloshes,/ As Susie steps slowly/ Along in the *slosh.*"[4] Sounds such as "k" and "g" give a harsh sound, as in Aldington's "Storm," also in *Time for Poetry:* "You crash over the trees,/ you crack the live branch."[5] Combinations of rhythm, rhyme, and repetition can give a sense of manipulation of ideas and language. For example, many of the poems in Dennis Lee's volume of poetry, *Alligator Pie,* are fanciful explorations of ideas and language.

Style. After having many experiences with language and literature, students can begin to understand style, which is the individual way authors express themselves in words and the way artists represent ideas in illustrations. Some authors and illustrators use several different styles; others use chiefly a single style and are recognized by it. Stories of nature told in verse remind one of Aileen Fisher. Humorous nonsense in rhyme and cartoonlike illustrations bring Dr. Seuss to mind. Sendak's little boys with turned-up mouths are readily recognizable as his invention. Zemach's illustrations are cluttered, intricate, and often humorous.

Recognizes Characteristics of Different Types of Literature

As students become familiar with different types of literature, they can begin to understand the distinguishing features that characterize particular forms. For example, poetry utilizes the sounds of languages (rhythm, rhyme, and repetition) to convey clear and strong messages. The elements of imagery and figurative language also contribute to its vividness and power. Ideas expressed through poetry take many forms and points of view. Judith Thurman in her book *Flashlight* describes poetry in this way:

A good poem is a flashlight . . . the flashlight of surprise. Pointed at a skinned knee or at an oil slick, at pretending to sleep or at kisses, at balloons, or snow, or at the soft, scary nuzzle of a mare, a poem lets us feel and know each in a fresh, sudden and strong light.[6]

Some of the features that make stories humorous are an amusing use of words, funny characters, surprising ideas, and chaotic and ridiculous situations. Alliteration, nonsense words, words with double meanings, puns, alteration of names, and misuse of big words lend to the humor of a story.[7]

Relates Elements to One Another

An important aspect of interpretation is relating the various elements in a work to one another. The conclusions drawn from making such relationships can often add another dimension of meaning to the work.

Relates characters and actions to plot. In the fantasy *Dragon Song,* by McCaffrey, different character roles are defined by their sex and position in the culture, and these roles affect their actions. In Cunningham's *Come to the Edge,* the boy establishes different relationships with the characters he meets on the basis of what they want him to be. Students can be guided to make conclusions about the relationship of the boy to each adult. In the picture books *Little Wood Duck,* by Wildsmith, and *Swimmy* and *Frederick,* by Lionni, the relationship of the characters and their actions can be noted and compared, with the conclusion that each character has something to contribute. These books could be contrasted with the picture books *Petunia,* by Duvoisin, and *Dazzle,* by Massie, in which the characters have a distorted opinion of their worth and as a result encounter difficulties.

Predicts outcomes and forms conclusions. Stories with surprise endings can be used to assist students in predicting outcomes. For example, part of Mayer's *Mrs. Beggs and the Wizard* can be read, and the ending of the story can be predicted. Students need to be helped to keep their predictions consistent with the characters and actions of the stories. The ending of O'Brien's *Mrs. Frisby and the Rats of NIMH* seems to be open for a sequel. Students might predict what will happen to the band of animals after they have established a new home in the valley. Books in a series can offer opportunities to predict outcomes and also increase motivation to read. Examples are the Forest Books, a historical fiction series by Barbara Willard, a science series by Snyder *(Below the Root, And All Between,* and *Until the Celebration),* and two science trilogies by Christopher *(The White Mountains, The City of Gold and Lead,* and *The Pool of Fire; The Prince in Waiting, Beyond the Burning Lands,* and *The Sword of the Spirit).*

Understands literary elements as clues to meaning. Older students can begin to understand that literary elements are clues to meaning. For example, repetition in *Millions of Cats,* by Gag, is used to emphasize the idea of how special the little cat was to be chosen by the old couple when there were "Cats here, cats there,/ Cats and kittens everywhere,/ Hundreds of cats,/ Thousands of cats,/ Millions and billions and trillions of cats."[8] Parallel plots and different points of view can be used to give a more complete understanding of an event, an experience, or a relationship. Mood, as depicted in the text and illustrations, can also enhance the meaning of a story.

Relates ideas to each other. Seeing relationships among ideas in works can assist students in understanding stories and poems. In the picture book *When the Sky Is Like Lace,* by Horwitz, the various activities in the story are related to the strong interests of children. The night is made magical partially because it offers fun activities for children. In

Byars' *The House of Wings* and Bulla's *White Bird,* a boy finds an injured bird. In *The House of Wings,* caring for the bird serves to bring the grandfather and boy together. In *White Bird,* a disagreement over whether or not to keep the injured bird causes a rift in the relationship between the boy and the man who has raised him.

In studying folk literature, common motifs that occur frequently, such as the evil wolf, the fairy godmother, and the magic pot, can be examined. Tales can also be studied for recurring patterns, such as the long sleep or enchantment, magical powers, magical transformations, magic objects, wishes, and trickery.[9] When studying motifs, it is interesting to take different versions of a common tale found in different parts of the world and to compare and contrast the motifs in them.

Two versions of the same story told through different media can be compared and contrasted. For example, students could discuss the effect of animation on *Charlotte's Web,* by E. B. White. In comparing the book version and the film version of Tolkien's *The Hobbits,* students could describe how their visualization of the hobbits differed from the film's portrayal of them.

A class of sixth graders read *The Mixed-Up Files of Mrs. Basil E. Frankweiler,* by Konigsburg, and then listened to the taped version. They decided that they enjoyed the story more after listening to the tape because the characters on the tape and the background music moved the story along at a faster pace and developed suspense.

Recognizes organizational patterns. Comparing the organizational patterns of different works may be a challenging experience for advanced students. After reading *Bridge to Terabithia,* by Paterson, and *Child of the Owl,* by Yep (volumes of realistic fiction) it can be concluded that the characters use fantasy to cope with the conflict in their lives. In *Bridge to Terabithia,* children meet in a secret place that is safe from the conflicts in their lives. They use their imaginations to become rulers of a magic kindgom. In *Child of the Owl,* the Chinese grandmother seeks to interpret her granddaughter's frustrations of moving from one culture to another. The child has been raised as an American and then goes to live in her grandmother's home, where she must adjust to traditional Chinese values. The grandmother relates her granddaughter's conflict to a story of owls that has a folk-tale quality. The grandmother explains to the girl that all people, just as Jasmine, the owl, have a longing to be free of cultural restraints and to exercise their individuality.

Interesting similarities can be noted in the organization of full-circle plots in folk tales. In this type of organization, the two extremes of a concept are explored, such as poverty and riches, little and big, lowly and powerful. In Hoffman's *Hans in Luck,* the boy starts out with nothing, receives a bag of gold, and ends up with nothing. In Brown's *Once a Mouse,* the mouse becomes as large as a tiger and then returns to being a mouse. The lowly stonecutter, in McDermott's *The Stonecutter,* wishes and receives more and more power until he is humbled again.

When discussing the organizational patterns of stories, teachers need to be aware that children under the age of eleven usually do not understand space and time concepts unless they are related to their own experiences. Flashbacks in fiction may not be understood by children who cannot deal intellectually with time beyond their own experience.

Considers Elements and Parts as They Relate
to the Meaning of the Whole Work

In the picture book *Dandelion,* by Freeman, the character's developments, his actions, and the different moods of the story can be related to the theme of the book: It is best to be yourself. In the beginning of the story, Dandelion is being himself; the mood of the story is cheerful and positive. Then he receives an invitation to Jennifer Giraffe's party; he gets a new hairdo and buys a new outfit to become a stylish dandy. The story takes on an exciting mood. When Dandelion goes to the party, Jennifer will not let him in because she does not recognize him. In his disappointment, he wanders about and gets caught in a rainstorm, which spoils his dandy appearance. This part of the story is filled with pathos. Then Dandelion pulls himself together and makes another attempt to go to the party. This time Jennifer recognizes him, and he is admitted to the party. The mood is happy again.

In the picture book *When the Sky Is Like Lace,* by Horwitz, the illustrations and the different aspects of the text contribute to making night a magical experience. The activities to do at night are ones that are enjoyed by children. These activities are made vivid and intensely exciting through the use of imagery, figurative language, and the word "bimulous," an invented word whose meaning the story makes clear. The repetition, rhythm, and rhyme schemes also offer an invitation to participate in this fun experience.

The relationship of character and plot development to the theme of Wier's *The Loner* is shown on the chart in Appendix Q. By noting the sequence of ideas and the change in the character, David, one can conclude that the character development is related to the theme of growing up.

Detects Relationships Between Characters as Reflections of Meaning

In some works, understanding the relationships between characters facilitates comprehending the theme. For example, in Lionni's *Frederick,* the relationship of the mouse, Frederick, to the working mice contributes to the theme that "man cannot live by bread alone." In Cunningham's book *Come to the Edge,* the relationship of the boy to each of the people who take him in indicates his lack of self-esteem. He allows all of these people to manipulate him to their own advantage so they will not discover that he is a rejected person.

Understands the Contributions of Different Types of Literature
to the Understanding of an Idea or a Concept

Choosing a topic of interest for students to study is one way to help them perceive how different types of literature can contribute to the understanding of an idea. An example might be a recent tornado in the community. Different types of literature concerning wind storms could be presented to illustrate that they give different perspectives and different degrees of objectivity to ideas and events. (See Appendix P, Library References of Children's Literature.) Examples of different types of literature are given below.

- Newspaper accounts

  A secondhand account of a disaster that occurred a thousand miles away

  A firsthand account of a reporter representing the state's largest newspaper

  A firsthand account of a local reporter

  A firsthand account reported by a victim of the storm

- Factual books written by professional meteorologists and scientific journalists
- Books of realistic fiction that manipulate elements and parts of a story to develop an idea
- Books of fantasy which are grounded in reality but which lead readers to consider ideas that they might not be able to face in reality
- Poems that create strong, vivid impressions of the idea or event through the use of the sound of language, imagery, and figurative language

Sees Different Levels of Meaning in a Work

Some works have more than one level of understanding, either intended by the author or inferred by the audience. Certain parts of a work may be open to more than one level of interpretation, such as the dog and the albatross in Speer's *Call It Courage.* The former represents friendship and constant support, and the latter suggests a warning of danger. In Lynd's *The Silver Pony,* the winged pony in the air represents the boy's flights of imagination.

In other instances the whole work can be considered on more than one level. For example, the picture book *Swimmy* can be viewed as a story about a small black fish who survives predators and then leads other fish to save themselves from being eaten. On another level, however, Swimmy represents a leader with ingenuity who offers to take charge of a vulnerable group.

Recognizes the Intention of an Author

Examining the messages interwoven in a work, the form of literature used as a medium, and the elements chosen to relay ideas can extend understanding and appreciation of literature. Such an examination can also make students more aware of the craft involved in using spoken and written language and in illustrating.

The intentions of authors can be speculated upon, and students can also get acquainted with their actual intentions. Librarians can be asked to assist in collecting newspaper and journal articles about authors, illustrators, and their works. There are also several collections about authors and illustrators available. A list of collections is given in Appendix T.

Students can write letters to the author or the publisher. Sometimes the publisher's reply will include a form letter from the author or illustrator or an article about his/her life and work. Some authors and illustrators will reply directly to the student. Teachers need to guide students, whose inquiries should reflect a genuine interest and knowledge of the author's or illustrator's works, not a letter-writing assignment. Students should be encouraged to share their letters with peers and teachers to ensure that all pertinent questions are included. Copies of the responses received can be compiled to make a source book for the school or classroom.

Authors and illustrators who are visiting in the area can be asked to visit schools. Before the visit, children should become acquainted with the works of the guests and prepare questions to ask them. The guest might be asked for permission to record the presentation so it could be shared with other children.

In summary, discussions of a work should offer students opportunities to recognize relationships and patterns, different levels of meaning within a work, the contributions of different types of literature to a concept or idea, and the intention of an author. In raising the level of the discussion to interpretation, teachers need to pay close attention to the responses of students, which can provide a natural bridge to higher-level tasks. The following remarks refer to reading books but could also apply to viewing and listening.

"I could not put the book down."
"I had goose flesh while I read the book."
"I read that book last year; I know I will never forget it."
"I've read four books in that series and cannot remember any of the stories."
"When I finished the book, I had a lump in my throat."
"It's the funniest book I have ever read."
"I would like to find more books by that author."
"I read the first book, and now I want to read the sequel."
"I would know the characters in the book if they walked into the room."
"This book reminds me of the book the teacher read to us."
"I like historical fiction best."

Affective Tasks and School Experiences

Affective tasks on the interpretation level are as follows:

A. Relates the work to personal experiences and knowledge of the world
B. Understands values within the work
C. Relates ideas and values in the work to ideas and values in other works

Students can perform these tasks if they have had a wide range of experiences with literature and with social-personal relationships. Comparing and contrasting ideas and values from different works and types of literature and relating them to personal experiences can serve to clarify students' understanding of themselves, others, and the world around them.

Affective tasks on this level involve understanding conflicts with self and with others. Students can learn about conflicts from many sources: television news programs and documentaries, newspaper and magazine articles, nonfiction books, diaries, and biographies as well as different types of fiction and poetry. For example, they could begin by studying various holocausts throughout history, such as the attempt of the Pol Pot regime to liquidate the educated in Cambodia. Other holocausts and the conflicting values behind them could be studied. A recently published biography by Kheridan, *The Road From Home,* tells of the Turks' attempt to destroy the Armenians in the early part of the twentieth century. Many factual and fictionalized accounts can be found of the Nazi attack against Jewish people and other ethnic groups in the 1930's and 1940's. By examining these events, students can begin to understand the great personal tragedy of individuals when they lose their rights of cultural, ethnic, and racial identity.

Students can explore in different works the conflicts of individuals with themselves. In Dickinson's *Annerton Pit* and Farrar's *Samantha on the Stage,* the main characters discover that they have conflicts with themselves as well as with others.

Conflicts with others can be explored from many vantage points, such as the various aspects of friendships. In Burch's *Wilken's Ghost,* the boy's friendship is betrayed. Jessica in Sachs' *A Secret Friend* finds that friendship involves loyalty as well as exciting experiences. In Greene's *Your Old Pal, Al,* friendships are subject to change. Through the process of living, new relationships are formed, and established ones may be altered. Susie in Shura's *The Season of Silence* finds that after a period of isolation because of an illness, many of her relationships with others have changed. Students can broaden their understanding of the many facets of friendship by discussing the various books they have read on the subject.

When individuals impose certain roles on others, a potential conflict is created. In Hooks' *Doug Meets the Nutcracker* and Simon's *A Special Gift,* the boys' involvement in ballet causes much conflict between them and their peers and some adults in their lives. The conflict that girls and young women have experienced throughout history in expressing their individuality can be found in many works of historical, realistic, and fantasy literature. Examples are Willard's *The Lark and the Laurel,* set in sixteenth century England; Lampman's *Bargain Bride,* set in the Oregon territory in the nineteenth century; Branscum's *Johnny May,* Rabe's *Naomi,* and Thrasher's *The Dark Didn't Catch Me,* all set in the era of the Great Depression; and the fantasy world of McCaffrey's *Dragon Song.* The picture book *Frederick,* by Lionni, presents the conflict between different roles. Working mice attend to matters of physical survival, an immediate and a crucial need, and the poet-philosopher mouse cares for the survival of the spirit.

Young people struggling to cope with the clashing values of adults in their lives is another example of conflict with others. In Barford's *Let Me Hear the Music,* the girl is confronted with a situation in which the boy's aunts bought shoes for him to be buried in, but did not buy them for him while he was alive. In *Dinah, Blow Your Horn,* by Bickham, the boy has difficulty understanding his father's loyalty to a company which is unfair to its workers. The boy in Angell's *A Word From Our Sponsor or My Friend Alfred* has a conflict with his father over his role in advertising a harmful product. The orphan boy in Avi's *Night Journey* has a conflict with his foster father, a Quaker opposed to slavery, when the father is pressed into finding runaway slaves.

Individuals caught between two cultures provide another example of conflict. Yep's *Child of the Owl* and George's *Julia of the Wolves* contain such conflicts. In *Child of the Owl,* a girl who has been raised as an American goes to live with her grandmother, whose life is governed by traditional Chinese values. Julia, in *Julia of the Wolves,* finds both the values of Eskimos and white people imposed on her. The confrontation of young people from different cultures is another perspective of human conflict, as seen in St. George's *The Halo Wind.*

The world around people can also bring about conflict. The hurricane in Hale's *The Night of the Hurricane* causes conflicts to surface among people and later causes them to recognize a common goal. In Barford's *Let Me Hear the Music,* the Depression causes personal disintegration but also forces people to call on inner strengths to make hard decisions.

When studying a particular conflict, students gain an in-depth understanding of it by reading and discussing several works that deal with different aspects of the same problem and present a wide range of perspectives.

Notes

1. Barbara Scott, a sixth-grade teacher at Squaw Creek School, Cedar Rapids, shared this experience.
2. Elinor Lander Horwitz, *When the Sky Is Like Lace,* illus. Barbara Cooney (Philadelphia: J. B. Lippincott Company, 1975), unpaged.
3. Carl Sandburg, "Fog," in *Time for Poetry,* compil. May Hill Arbuthnot and Shelton L. Root, Jr. (3rd ed.; Chicago: Scott, Foresman and Company, 1968), p. 171.
4. Rhoda W. Bacmeister, "Galoshes," in *Time for Poetry,* p. 167.
5. Hilda Doolittle Aldington, "Storm," in *Time for Poetry,* p. 166.
6. Judith Thurman, *Flashlight* (New York: Atheneum, 1976), jacket of book.
7. Dianne Monson, "What's So Funny?" *Early Years,* VII (February, 1977), pp. 26–29.
8. Wanda Gag, *Millions of Cats* (New York: Coward, McCann, 1928), unpaged.
9. Charolotte S. Huck, *Children's Literature in the Elementary School* (3rd ed. update; New York: Holt, Rinehart and Winston, 1979), pp. 170–73.

Bibliography

Angell, Judi. *A Word From Our Sponsor or My Friend Alfred.* Scarsdale, N.Y.: Bradbury Press, 1979.

Arbuthnot, May Hill and Shelton L. Root, Jr., compil. *Time for Poetry.* 3rd ed. Chicago: Scott, Foresman and Company, 1968.

Arbuthnot, May Hill and Mark Taylor. *Time for Old Magic.* Chicago: Scott, Foresman and Company, 1970.

Avi. *Night Journey.* New York: Pantheon Books, 1979.

Barford, Carol. *Let Me Hear the Music.* New York: Seabury Press, 1979.

Baylor, Byrd. *Guess Who My Favorite Person Is,* illus. Robert Andrew Parker. New York: Charles Scribner's Sons, 1977.

————. *The Other Way to Listen,* illus. Peter Parnall. New York: Charles Scribner's Sons, 1978.

Belting, Natalia. *The Wind Is a Ghost Dancing,* illus. Leo and Diane Dillon. New York: E. P. Dutton and Company, 1974.

Bickham, Jack M. *Dinah, Blow Your Horn.* Garden City, N.Y.: Doubleday and Company, 1979.

Blos, Joan W. *A Gathering of Days.* New York: Charles Scribner's Sons, 1979.

Branscum, Robbie. *Johnny May.* Garden City, N.Y.: Doubleday and Company, 1975.

Brown, Marcia. *Once a Mouse.* New York: Charles Scribner's Sons, 1961.

Bulla, Clyde Robert. *White Bird.* New York: Thomas Y. Crowell Company, 1966.

Burch, Robert. *Wilkin's Ghost.* New York: Viking Press, 1978.

Burningham, John. *Come Away From the Water, Shirley.* New York: Thomas Y. Crowell Company, 1977.

Byars, Betsy. *The House of Wings*. New York: Viking Press, 1972.
Christopher, John. *Beyond the Burning Lands*. New York: Macmillan Publishing Company, 1970.
————. *The City of Gold and Lead*. New York: Macmillan Publishing Company, 1967.
————. *The Pool of Fire*. New York: Macmillan Publishing Company, 1968.
————. *The Prince in Waiting*. New York: Macmillan Publishing Company, 1970.
————. *The Sword of the Spirit*. New York: Macmillan Publishing Company, 1972.
————. *The White Mountains*. New York: Macmillan Publishing Company, 1967.
Cunningham, Julia. *Come to the Edge*. New York: Pantheon Books, 1977.
Dickinson, Peter. *Annerton Pit*. Boston: Little, Brown and Company, 1977.
Duvoisin, Roger. *Petunia*. New York: Alfred A. Knopf, 1950.
Farrar, Susan Clement. *Samantha on Stage*. New York: Dial Press, 1979.
Freeman, Don. *Dandelion*. New York: Harper and Row, 1965.
Gág, Wanda. *Millions of Cats*. New York: Coward-McCann, 1928.
George, Jean Craighead. *Julia of the Wolves*. New York: Harper and Row, 1972.
Greene, Constance C. *Your Old Pal, Al*. New York: Viking Press, 1979.
Greenfield, Eloise. *Honey, I Love*, illus. Leo and Diane Dillon. New York: Thomas Y. Crowell Company, 1978.
Gripe, Maria. *Julia's House*. New York: Delacorte Press, 1971.
Hale, Nancy. *The Night of the Hurricane*. New York: Coward, McCann and Geoghegan, 1978.
Härtling, Peter. *Oma*. New York: Delacorte Press, 1971.
Heide, Florence Perry. *Banana Twist*. New York: Holiday House, 1978.
Hickman, Janet. *The Stones*. New York: Macmillan Publishing Company, 1976.
Hoffman, Felix. *Hans in Luck*. New York: Atheneum, 1975.
Hooks, William. *Doug Meets the Nutcracker*. New York: Frederick Warne, 1977.
Horwitz, Elinor. *When the Sky Is Like Lace*, illus. Barbara Cooney. Philadelphia: J. B. Lippincott Company, 1975.
Huck, Charlotte S. *Children's Literature in the Elementary School*. 3rd ed. update. New York: Holt, Rinehart and Winston, 1979.
Hunter, Mollie. *The Third Eye*. New York: Harper and Row, 1979.
Kheridan, David. *The Road From Home*. New York: William Morrow and Company, 1979.
Konigsburg, E. L. *Father's Arcane Daughter*. New York: Atheneum, 1976.
————. *The Mixed-Up Files of Mrs. Basil E. Frankweiler*. New York: Atheneum, 1969.
Lampman, Evelyn Sibley. *Bargain Bride*. New York: Atheneum, 1977.
Lee, Dennis. *Alligator Pie*. Boston: Houghton Mifflin Company, 1975.
Lionni, Leo. *Frederick*. New York: Pantheon Books, 1967.
————. *Swimmy*. New York: Pantheon Books, 1963.
Livingston, Myra Cohn. *4-Way Stop*. New York: Atheneum, 1976.
Massie, Diane. *Dazzle*. New York: Parents' Magazine Press, 1969.
Mayer, Mercer. *Mrs. Beggs and the Wizard*. New York: Parents' Magazine Press, 1973.
McCaffrey, Anne. *Dragon Song*. New York: Atheneum, 1976.
McCloskey, Robert. *Time of Wonder*. New York: Viking Press, 1957.
McDermott, Gerald. *The Stonecutter*. New York: Viking Press, 1975.
Monson, Dianne. "What's So Funny?" *Early Years*, VII (February, 1977), 26–29.
O'Brien, Robert. *Mrs. Frisby and the Rats of NIMH*. New York: Atheneum, 1971.
Paterson, Katherine. *Bridge to Terabithia*. New York: Thomas Y. Crowell Company, 1977.
————. *The Great Gilly Hopkins*. New York: Thomas Y. Crowell Company, 1978.
Peck, Robert Newton. *Soup*. New York: Alfred A. Knopf, 1974.
Rabe, Berniece. *Naomi*. Nashville: Thomas Nelson, 1975.
Rodgers, Mary. *Freaky Friday*. New York: Harper and Row, 1972.
Sachs, Marilyn. *A Secret Friend*. Garden City, N.Y.: Doubleday and Company, 1978.
St. George, Judith. *The Halo Wind*. New York: G. P. Putnam's Sons, 1978.

Shector, Ben. *Conrad's Castle.* New York: Harper and Row, 1979.

Shura, Mary Francis. *The Season of Silence.* New York: Atheneum, 1976.

Simon, Marcia L. *A Special Gift.* New York: Harcourt Brace Jovanovich, 1978.

Smith, James Steele. *A Critical Approach to Children's Literature.* New York: McGraw-Hill Book Company, 1967.

Sperry, Armstrong. *Call It Courage.* New York: Macmillan Publishing Company, 1941.

Snyder, Zilpha Keatley. *And All Between.* New York: Atheneum, 1976.

———— . *Below the Root.* New York: Atheneum, 1975.

———— . *Until the Celebration.* New York: Atheneum, 1977.

Thrasher, Crystal. *The Dark Didn't Catch Me.* New York: Atheneum, 1975.

Thurman, Judith. *Flashlight.* New York: Atheneum, 1976.

Tolkien, J. R. R. *The Hobbits.* Boston: Houghton Mifflin Company, 1938.

Tresselt, Alvin. *What Did You Leave Behind?* illus. Roger Duvoisin. New York: Lothrop, Lee and Shephard, 1978.

Twain, Mark. *The Adventures of Tom Sawyer.* New York: Harper and Brothers, 1875.

VonCannon, Claudia. *The Moonclock.* Boston: Houghton Mifflin Company, 1979.

Ward, Lynd. *The Silver Pony.* Boston: Houghton Mifflin Company, 1973.

White, E. B. *Charlotte's Web.* New York: Harper and Row, 1952.

Wier, Ester. *The Loner.* New York: David McKay Company, 1963.

Wilder, Laura Ingalls. *On the Banks of Plum Creek.* New York: Harper and Row, 1937.

Wildsmith, Brian. *Little Wood Duck.* New York: Franklin Watts, 1973.

Willard, Barbara. *A Cold Wind Blows.* New York: E. P. Dutton and Company, 1973.

———— . *The Iron Lily.* New York: E. P. Dutton and Company, 1974.

———— . *The Lark and the Laurel.* New York: E. P. Dutton and Company, 1970.

———— . *The Sprig of Broom.* New York: E. P. Dutton and Company, 1972.

Yep, Lawrence. *Child of the Owl.* New York: Harper and Row, 1977.

Yolen, Jane. *The Seeing Stick,* illus. Remy Charlip and Demetra Maraslis. New York: Thomas Y. Crowell Company, 1977.

Zemach, Margot. *It Could Always Be Worse.* New York: Farrar, Straus and Giroux, 1976.

Evaluation

The process of evaluation involves establishing a set of criteria that serve as a basis for judging a work. In order to do this, students need to be able to think logically, to cope with other points of view, to establish their own value system on a conscious level, and to have had many experiences with language and literature on the attending, literal understanding, and interpretation levels.

The tasks of evaluation, or critical thinking, encompass the cognitive and affective domains. They are as follows:

I. Cognitive tasks
    A. Establishes criteria as means to judge work
        1. Establishes criteria of form
        2. Establishes criteria of content
    B. Compares the work to others of its kind
II. Affective tasks
    A. Uses own value system to judge work
    B. Re-examines own responses to the work in light of responses of others

Even though higher levels of development and an extensive background of experiences with language are needed to effectively engage in the tasks of evaluation, teachers can assist children in examining works long before the students are capable of developing adequate sets of criteria. For example, kindergarten children can be asked what they liked about a book or a television program or which book or television program they liked best and why. Due to their level of development and degree of experience, their responses will not reflect logical, flexible thinking or an understanding of the point of view of others. Even so, these children are gaining experience in thinking about the worth of a work in light of its meaning to them.

The rapport teachers establish with students facilitates the development of evaluation abilities. The morning after the first program of the television series *Roots* was broadcast, two third-grade boys enthusiastically asked their teacher if she had seen the program. Although the teacher had been unable to watch the program, she asked the boys to tell her what they thought was good about the show. They responded by recalling exciting events, and finally one of the boys said he liked the program because it was about black people. These boys had viewed and listened to ideas with which they could closely associate. They had found themselves in the program.

Teachers can sometimes encourage reluctant older students to read by tapping their interests. At the beginning of the school year, Matthew, a fourth grader, informed his teacher that there were no good books, and that he did not like to read. As the year progressed, he avoided reading and got more frustrated about his lack of progress in reading class. The teacher found in the public library a simple book on wrestling with many illustrations. She recalled that Matthew was into his second year of wrestling at the YMCA and was extremely proud of what he had accomplished. The teacher checked out the book and asked Matthew to review it for her. She asked him to tell her if it was a good book on wrestling and if it should be on a list of recommended books on sports. After a week had passed, the teacher asked about the book. Matthew said that he had taken the book home, but he assured her that he was taking care of it. Matthew had read the book many times.

At an early age, children can begin to judge works for accuracy of content. For example, they can see if the text and illustrations of a book are consistent. In Bemelmans' *Madeline,* only eleven girls are brushing their teeth in the illustration while the text relates that there are twelve. Television programs too may provide examples of inaccuracies. A third-grade boy, after watching a program on the life of Martha Washington, checked some of the facts presented and found that they could not be substantiated. The producers had failed to tell the audience that the program was based on information that was generally accepted but not established fact.

In the primary years, children are also capable of understanding the support that illustrations give to the text of a picture book. For example, the cartoon characters in Seuss' books add to his lively, humorous stories. The dark, hazy illustrations in Shulevitz' *Dawn* underscore the quietness of this event.

As they develop and have experiences with literature, children can begin to recall favorite characters from stories and to understand why these characters are memorable. In primary years, children may enjoy Max, Madeline, Peter, and Petunia. In the middle elementary years, Frederick, Dandelion, Amos, and Pippi Longstockings may be favorites. Students in later elementary and junior high school may especially like Gilly, Soup and Robert, and the Hobbits. Fine character delineation, by providing pleasure, interest, and understanding of motives and conflicts, makes the experience memorable.

To judge the form of a work, the criteria need to be specific to a certain type of literature. In judging historical fiction, one must consider the authenticity with which the author presents the particular period. In realistic fiction the motives of the characters and the sequence of events need to be probable and follow a logical development. Modern fantasy must be firmly grounded in reality before taking the leap to the fanciful. Poetry should express ideas and feelings in a vivid and intense way and provoke strong emotional responses. Criteria for the evaluation of different types of literature are presented in Charlotte Huck's book, *Children's Literature in the Elementary School.*

Judging the accuracy and completeness of works can be facilitated by using several sources to study ideas, events, and issues. For this, students need to acquire reference skills. As children progress through elementary school, the daily discussion period, sometimes known as sharing time, needs to be more and more concerned with judging content. Students should begin to look for the intention, the objectivity, and the authority of the author. As they become more analytical in their thinking, they can select topics and issues to discuss in small groups and then share with the class. Their discussion should be based on information from many sources. These sources need to be noted and then compared and contrasted in the students' report on topics and issues.

Students of all ages are bombarded with media commercials which they must judge for accuracy and completeness. They can become more sophisticated in recognizing the techniques of persuasion used by advertising agencies. For primary-age children, food and toy commercials are interesting areas to study critically. A list of propaganda techniques used in advertising is given in Appendix U.

Young children can begin to compare works of specific types of literature. They can be asked to share their favorite animal characters from books in an independent learning center. The same assignment can be used with older students by having them select a specific type of book or television program and apply established criteria to the evaluation process.

Older students can establish awards for the best book and television program for the year or for the best ones in specific categories, based on established criteria. Students can make awards for the best books in different categories of fiction, published within the last five or ten years.

Works may meet criteria for content and form, which are cognitive aspects of evaluation, but may be rejected on the basis of criteria related to an individual's value system, the affective dimension of evaluation. The work may be well written but may violate a person's view of the meaning of life.

It can be both interesting and enlightening for students to share their evaluation of a work and then re-examine their own responses to the work in light of the responses of others. When re-examining one's own response to a work, a person may find that a positive or negative response may be given because of a close identification with the event or problem encountered in the work.

Bibliography

Bemelmans, Ludwig. *Madeline*. New York: Viking Press, 1939.

Emberley, Ed. *Green Says Go*. Boston: Little, Brown and Company, 1968.

Huck, Charlotte S. *Children's Literature in the Elementary School*. 3rd ed. update. New York: Holt, Rinehart and Winston, 1979.

Schlevitz, Uri. *Dawn*. New York: Farrar, Straus and Giroux, 1974.

Application

The application process, which involves both the cognitive and affective domains, includes the following tasks:

I. Cognitive tasks
   A. Generalizes from content to build a base for problem-solving strategies
   B. Generalizes from experiences with work(s) to develop effective techniques of expression
II. Affective tasks
   A. Relates values identified in a work to one's own and those of others
   B. Understands literature as a method of stating and exploring values; uses literature as a means to explore values
   C. Respects place of literature as a means to understanding
   D. Respects others' right to read
   E. Relates literature to other subjects and situations in life
   F. Moves from work to creative experiences

The mastery of the processes in the lower categories of comprehension (attention, literal understanding, interpretation, and evaluation) facilitates the use of the application processes. For example, in order to effectively generalize from sources to build a base for problem solving, it may be useful to judge the worth of works, an evaluation task, or to recognize the intention of the author, an interpretation task. The manipulation of explicit and implicit ideas from many sources as well as from different types of literature allows students to develop a base from which they can recognize and define problems; form tentative solutions; engage in the data-collecting, organizing, and interpreting processes; and form conclusions.

The application process involves thinking which starts from a common point and branches off. Students move beyond the ideas at hand to explore problems and propose solutions. After they have generalized from their viewing, listening, and reading experiences, they may use their imaginations to move beyond their immediate point in time and space to explore and discover something new to them. These explorations usually do not result in ideas that are original but may lead to seeing a relationship or synthesizing ideas to gain a new insight into a problem or process. Teachers can facilitate creative thinking by providing experiences that will extend students' horizons, sensitize them to events around them, and provide alternatives for expression. Teachers can also present experiences to more advanced students to develop an understanding that through the ages, people have used fantasy to explore human problems and the forces of nature. Examples of human exploration can be found in mythology and science fiction. Students can begin to understand that people imagined before they developed theoretical formulations.

On the application level, the tasks in the cognitive and affective domains frequently need to be performed simultaneously. Along with considering the "how" in application, students need to be aware of the "why." When developing an idea, students should consider if the outcome of the problem-solving process will be consistent with the individual's and society's values. For example, in space exploration both the cognitive and the affective need to be considered. How do we get there? Why are we going there? The conflict of the cognitive and the affective can be explored in factual and historical fiction accounts of great scientific and technological breakthroughs and biographies of great innovators.

In many instances, students progress from application tasks to composition; the fulfillment of the tasks leads naturally to the expression of the ideas generated by the application process. Teachers need to provide experiences in the content areas as well as in language arts and literature so students can explore different techniques of expression. By performing interpretation tasks, students can understand how literary elements and characteristics of different types of literature facilitate the expression of ideas. Teachers can present different ways to verbally compose ideas and to use other expressive forms such as art media, music, drama, and dance. An understanding of the different alternatives for expression may free students to engage in the application process.

Some of the affective tasks in the application process are related to controversial uses of literature. Tasks A, B, and C can lead children to be more aware of the conflicts of humans in dealing with themselves, others, and the forces of the universe. To some teachers, these tasks may imply bibliotherapy, which involves exploring in works the responses of others to social-emotional conflicts and then using these solutions to cope with problems. Little research is available to show how effective bibliotherapy is in influencing people's attitudes and behavior. Works that are didactic should not be presented to children; they do not like preaching. Teachers also should avoid using books as projective techniques. Such counseling sessions need to be left to specially prepared people.

Another controversial issue in literature is censorship, which is related to the task "respects others' right to read." Older students should begin to understand the difference between the evaluation of a literary work and censorship. Students need to understand the right of people in a free society to choose what they will view, listen to, and read.

Because today's children are exposed to conflict at an early age, the support of teachers and parents is more important than ever for their development. Teachers and parents should be aware of children's viewing, listening, and reading choices and give them opportunities to discuss their comprehension experiences. When students express an interest in records, television programs, and books, teachers can present works of high literary value that are related to the students' interests. Then they will have an opportunity to develop appreciation and a taste for good literature. The quickest way to encourage students to read works of poor quality is to disapprove of them. The best advertising that authors and publishing houses can obtain is to have their works published on a list of banned books.

Inherent in the tasks of application is the integration of the language arts. Various forms of composition are natural extensions of application tasks because comprehension and composition are an integral part of communication. The integration of the language arts should be achieved not only at the application level but on all levels of comprehension. Students view, listen, and read and then communicate ideas and feelings about their comprehension experiences. In each of the chapters on the different levels of comprehension, many examples of expressive activities related to literature experiences are presented. In Appendix I, a wide range of these activities is given for independent learning centers.

List of Appendices

Appendix A
Books for Young Children*

Adams, Florence. *Mushy Eggs*. New York: G.P. Putnam's Sons, 1973.

Adler, David A. *A Little at a Time,* illus. N.M. Bodecker. New York: Random House, 1976.

Ancona, George. *I Feel*. New York: E.P. Dutton and Company, 1977.

Andersen, Karen Born. *What's the Matter, Sylvie, Can't You Ride?* New York: Dial Press, 1981.

Annett, Cora. *The Dog Who Thought He Was a Boy,* illus. Walter Lorraine. Boston: Houghton Mifflin Company, 1965.

Asch, Frank. *Moon Bear*. New York: Charles Scribner's Sons, 1979.

———— . *Rebecka*. New York: Harper and Row, 1972.

———— . *Sand Cake*. New York: Parents' Magazine Press, 1978.

———— . *The Last Puppy*. Englewood Cliffs, N.J.: Prentice-Hall, 1980.

———— . *Turtle Tree*. New York: Dial Press, 1978.

Bang, Betsy. *The Old Woman and the Red Pumpkin,* illus. Molly Garrett. New York: Macmillan Publishing Company, 1975.

Barrett, Judi. *I Hate to Go to Bed*. New York: Four Winds Press, 1977.

Barton, Byron. *Buzz Buzz Buzz*. New York: Macmillan Publishing Company, 1973.

Becker, John. *Seven Little Rabbits,* illus. Barbara Cooney. New York: Walker and Company, 1973.

Behrens, June. *What I Hear in My School,* photo. Michele and Tom Grimm. Chicago: Children's Press, 1976.

Berson, Harold. *A Moose Is Not a Mouse*. New York: Crown Publishers, 1975.

Bornstein, Ruth Lercher. *Annabelle*. New York: Thomas Y. Crowell Company, 1978.

———— . *I'll Draw a Meadow*. New York: Harper and Row, 1979.

Brandenberg, Franz. *I Wish I Was Sick, Too!* illus. Aliki. New York: William Morrow and Company, 1976.

———— . *Nice New Neighbors*. New York: William Morrow and Company, 1977.

Brown, Marcia. *The Bun*. New York: Harcourt Brace Jovanovich, 1972.

Bunting, Eve. *Winter's Coming*. New York: Harcourt Brace Jovanovich, 1977.

Burningham, John. *Mr. Gumpy's Motor Car*. New York: Thomas Y. Crowell Company, 1976.

———— . *Mr. Gumpy's Outing*. New York: Holt, Rinehart and Winston, 1971.

———— . *Would You Rather . . .* New York: Thomas Y. Crowell Company, 1978.

Cartwright, Sally. *Sand*. New York: Coward, McCann and Geoghegan, 1975.

Chorao, Kay. *Lester's Overnight*. New York: E.P. Dutton and Company, 1977.

Clifton, Lucille. *Don't You Remember?* illus. Evaline Ness. New York: E.P. Dutton and Company, 1973.

———— . *Everett Anderson's 1, 2, 3,* illus. Ann Grifalconi. New York: Holt, Rinehart and Winston, 1977.

*Published since 1970

Craft, Ruth, and Erick Blegvad. *The Winter Bear*. New York: Atheneum, 1975.

Crowe, Robert. *Clyde Monster,* illus. Kay Chorao. New York: E.P. Dutton and Company, 1976.

Delton, Judy. *My Mom Hates Me in January*. Chicago: Albert Whitman and Company, 1977.

de Paola, Thomas. *Now One Foot, Now the Other*. New York: G.P. Putman's Sons, 1981.

de Paola, Tomie. *Nanna Upstairs and Nanna Downstairs*. New York: G.P. Putnam's Sons, 1973.

de Regniers, Beatrice Schenk. *It Does Not Say Meow and Other Animal Riddles,* illus. Paul Galdone. New York: Seabury Press, 1972.

———— . *Little Red Riding Hood,* illus. Edward Gorey. New York: Atheneum, 1972.

Domanska, Janina. *I Saw a Ship A-Sailing*. New York: Macmillan Publishing Company, 1972.

———— . *Spring Is*. New York: William Morrow and Company, 1976.

Duvoisin, Roger. *Jasmine*. New York: Alfred A. Knopf, 1973.

Elliott, Alan C. *On Sunday the Wind,* illus. Susan Bonners. New York: William Morrow and Company, 1980.

Fregosi, Claudia. *The Happy Horse*. New York: William Morrow and Company, 1977.

Freschet, Bernice. *The Web in the Grass,* illus. Roger Duvoisin. New York: Charles Scribner's Sons, 1972.

Friskey, Margaret. *Three Sides and the Round One*. Chicago: Children's Press, 1973.

Galdone, Joan. *The Tallypo,* illus. Paul Galdone. New York: Seabury Press, 1977.

Galdone, Paul. *The Three Bears*. New York: Seabury Press, 1972.

———— . *The Three Billy Goats Gruff*. New York: Seabury Press, 1973.

———— . *The Little Red Hen*. New York: Seabury Press, 1973.

Garelick, May. *Down to the Beach,* illus. Barbara Cooney. New York: Four Winds Press, 1973.

Gerson, Mary Joan. *Omateji's Baby Brother,* illus. Elzia Moon. New York: Henry Z. Walck, 1974.

Getz, Arthur. *Tar Beach*. New York: Dial Press, 1979.

Ginsburg, Mirra. *The Strongest One of All,* illus. Jose Aruego and Ariane Dewey. New York: William Morrow and Company, 1977.

Glasgow, Aline. *Honsehi,* illus. Tony Chen. New York: Parents' Magazine Press, 1972.

Goffstein, M.B. *Fish for Supper*. New York: Dial Press, 1976.

Goodall, John S. *Shrewbettina's Birthday*. New York: Harcourt Brace Jovanovich, 1971.

———— . *The Midnight Adventures of Kelly, Dot and Esmeralda*. New York: Atheneum, 1972.

Graham, Margaret Bloy. *Benjy's Dog House*. New York: Harper and Row, 1973.

Greenberg, Barbara. *The Bravest Babysitter,* illus. Diane Paterson. New York: Dial Press, 1977.

Hamberger, John. *The Sleepless Day*. New York: Four Winds Press, 1973.

Hann, Jacquie. *Crybaby*. New York: Four Winds Press, 1979.

Hapgood, Miranda. *Martha's Bad Day*. New York: Crown Publishers, 1977.

Harper, Anita. *How We Live,* illus. Christina Roche. New York: Harper and Row, 1977.

Hatch, Shirley Cook. *Wind Is To Feel*. New York: Coward, McCann and Geoghegan, 1973.

Hazen, Barbara Shook. *Tight Times,* illus. Trina Schart Hyman. New York: Viking Press, 1979.

———— . *Where Do Bears Sleep?* illus. Ian E. Staunton. Reading, Mass.: Addison-Wesley, 1970.

Heller, Linda. *Lily at the Table*. New York: Macmillan Publishing Company, 1979.

Hoban, Russell. *Egg Thoughts and Other Frances Songs,* illus. Lillian Hoban. New York: Harper and Row, 1972.

Hurd, Edith Thacher. *Johnny Lion's Bad Day,* illus. Clement Hurd. New York: Harper and Row, 1970.

———— . *Johnny Lion's Rubber Boats*. New York: Harper and Row, 1972.

Hutchins, Pat. *Changes, Changes*. New York: Macmillan Publishing Company, 1971.

———— . *The Wind Blew*. New York: Macmillan Publishing Company, 1974.

———— . *Titch*. New York: Macmillan Publishing Company, 1971.

Hutton, Warwick. *Noah and the Great Flood*. New York: Atheneum, 1977.

Ichikawa, Satomi. *A Child's Book of Seasons*. New York: Parents' Magazine Press, 1975.

Isadore, Rachel. *Willaby*. New York: Macmillan Publishing Company, 1977.

Jeffers, Susan. *Three Jovial Huntsmen*. Scarsdale, N.Y.: Bradbury Press, 1973.

Jewell, Nancy. *Calf, Goodnight,* illus. Leonard Weisgard. New York: Harper and Row, 1973.

Junes, Penelope. *I'm Not Moving*. Scarsdale, N.Y.: Bradbury Press, 1980.

Keats, Ezra Jack. *Pet Show*. New York: Macmillan Publishing Company, 1972.

———— . *Over in the Meadow*. New York: Four Winds Press, 1971.

Kellogg, Steven. *Can I Keep Him?* New York: Dial Press, 1971.

———— . *Pinkerton, Behave!* New York: Dial Press, 1979.

———— . *The Mystery of the Missing Red Mitten*. New York: Dial Press, 1974.

Kessler, Ethel and Leonard Kessler. *Slush Slush!* New York: Parents' Magazine Press, 1973.

Kishido, Erico. *The Lion and the Bird's Nest,* illus. Chiyoko Nakatani. New York: Thomas Y. Crowell Company, 1972.

Kohn, Bernice. *How High Is Up?* illus. Jan Pyk. New York: G.P. Putnam's Sons, 1971.

Kraus, Robert. *Kittens for Nothing,* illus. Diane Paterson, New York: E.P. Dutton and Company, 1976.

Kroll, Steven. *The Tyrannosaurus Game,* illus. Tomie de Paola. New York: Holiday House, 1976.

Kuratomi, Chizuko. *Mr. Bear and the Robbers,* illus. Kozo Kakimoto. New York: Dial Press, 1970.

Kuskin, Karla. *A Boy Had a Mother Who Bought Him a Hat*. Boston: Houghton Mifflin Company, 1976.

Lasky, Kathryn. *I Have Four Names for My Grandfather,* photo. Christopher G. Knight. Boston: Little, Brown and Company, 1976.

Lear, Edward. *Whizz!* New York: Macmillan Publishing Company, 1973.

Lippman, Peter. *Busy Wheels*. New York: Random House, 1973.

Lobel, Arnold. *On Market Street,* illus. Anita Lobel. New York: Greenwillow Books, 1981.

Mayer, Mercer. *Bubble Bubble.* New York: Parents' Magazine Press, 1973.

———— . *Frog on His Own.* New York: Dial Press, 1973.

———— . *Just For You.* New York: Golden Press, 1975.

McLeod, Emilie Warren. *The Bear's Bicycle.* Boston: Little, Brown and Company, 1975.

Merriam, Eve. *Unhurry Harry,* illus. Gail Owens. New York: Four Winds Press, 1978.

Miles, Miska. *Chicken Forgets,* illus. Jim Arnosky. Boston: Little, Brown and Company, 1976.

———— . *Small Rabbit,* illus. Jim Arnosky. Boston: Little, Brown and Company, 1977.

———— . *Swim, Little Duck,* illus. Jim Arnosky. Boston: Little, Brown and Company, 1976.

Miller, Edna. *Duck, Duck.* New York: Holiday House, 1971.

Mitchell, Cynthia. *Playtime,* illus. Satomi Ichikawa. New York: Collins, 1978.

Moffett, Martha. *A Flower Pot Is Not a Hat,* illus. Susan Perl. New York: E.P. Dutton and Company, 1972.

Montresor, Beni. *Bedtime.* New York: Harper and Row, 1978.

Myers, Amy. *I Know a Monster.* Reading, Mass.: Addison-Wesley, 1979.

Nixon, Joan Lowery. *The Alligator Under the Bed,* illus. Jan Hughes. New York: G.P. Putnam's Sons, 1974.

Noble, Trinka Hakes. *The Day Jimmy's Boa Ate the Wash,* illus. Steven Kellogg. New York: Dial Press, 1980.

Paterson, Diane. *If I Were a Toad.* New York: Dial Press, 1977.

Patz, Nancy. *Pumpernickel Tickle and Mean Green Cheese.* New York: Franklin Watts, 1978.

Plath, Sylvia. *The Bed Book,* illus. Emily Arnold McCully. New York: Harper and Row, 1976.

Pomerantz, Charlotte. *The Mango Tooth,* illus. Marilyn Hafner. New York: William Morrow and Company, 1977.

Provensen, Alice, and Martin Provensen. *My Little Hen.* New York: Random House, 1973.

Raskin, Ellen. *Who, Said Sue, Said Whoo?* New York: Random House, 1973.

Rice, Eve. *Oh, Lewis.* New York: Macmillan Publishing Company, 1974.

Richer, Mischa. *Quack?* New York: Harper and Row, 1978.

Rockwell, Anne. *The Awful Mess.* New York: Parents' Magazine Press, 1973.

———— . *The Gallywhopper Egg.* New York: Macmillan Publishing Company, 1974.

Rockwell, Anne, and Harlow Rockwell. *Machines.* New York: Macmillan Publishing Company, 1972.

Romanek, Enid Warner. *Teddy.* New York: Charles Scribner's Sons, 1978.

Roy, Ron. *Three Ducks Went Wandering,* illus. Paul Galdone. New York: Seabury Press, 1979.

Ryan, Cheli Duran. *Hildilid's Night,* illus. Arnold Lobel. New York: Macmillan Publishing Company, 1971.

Schlein, Miriam. *The Way Mothers Are.* Chicago: Albert Whitman and Company, 1974.

Scott, Ann Herbert. *On Mother's Lap,* illus. Glo Coalson. New York: McGraw-Hill Book Company, 1972.

Sendak, Maurice. *Seven Little Monsters*. New York: Harper and Row, 1975.

Shapiro, Irwin. *Twice Upon a Time,* illus. Adrienne Adams. New York: Charles Scribner's Sons, 1973.

Sharmat, Marjorie, and Mitchell Sharmat. *I Am Not a Pest,* illus. Diane Dawson. New York: E.P. Dutton and Company, 1979.

Sharmat, Mitchell. *Gregory, The Terrible Eater,* illus. Jose Aruego and Ariane Dewey. New York: Four Winds Press, 1980.

Singer, Marilyn. *The Pickle Pan,* illus. Steven Kellogg. New York: E.P. Dutton and Company, 1978.

Smith, Mr. and Mrs. *The Long Slide*. New York: Atheneum, 1977.

Srvilich, Sandra Stroner. *I'm Going on a Bear Hunt,* illus. Glen Rounds. New York: E.P. Dutton and Company, 1973.

Stevens, Carla. *Stories from a Snowy Meadow*. New York: Four Winds Press, 1976.

Stroschin, J. H. *The Cloudy Day*. South Bend, Ind.: Regnery/Gateway, 1979.

Thayer, Jane. *Applebaum's Have a Robot,* illus. Bari Weissman. New York: William Morrow and Company, 1980.

Tobias, Tabi. *A Day Off*. New York: G.P. Putnam's Sons, 1973.

———— . *Moving Day,* illus. William Pène du Bois, New York: Alfred A. Knopf, 1976.

Tresselt, Alvin. *What Did You Leave Behind?* illus. Roger Duvoisin. New York: Lothrop, Lee and Shephard, 1978.

Ueno, Noriko. *Elephant Buttons*. New York: Harper and Row, 1973.

Viorst, Judith. *My Mamma Says*. New York: Atheneum, 1973.

Wahl, Jan. *Dracula's Cat,* illus. Kay Chorao. Englewood Cliffs, N.J.: Prentice-Hall, 1978.

Warach, Marie Norkin. *I Like Red*. New York: Dandelion Press, 1979.

Watson, Clyde. *Catch Me and Kiss Me and Say It Again,* illus. Wendy Watson. New York: Collins, 1978.

———— . *Lollipop*. New York: Thomas Y. Crowell Company, 1976.

Weil, Liel. *Fat Ernest*. New York: Parents' Magazine Press, 1973.

Wells, Rosemary. *Noisy Nora*. New York: Dial Press, 1973.

———— . *Unfortunately Harriett*. New York: Dial Press, 1972.

Westerberg, Christine. *The Cap That Mother Made*. Englewood Cliffs, N.J.: Prentice-Hall, 1977.

Wildsmith, Brian. *The Little Wood Duck*. New York: Franklin Watts, 1973.

———— . *Puzzles*. New York: Franklin Watts, 1970.

———— . *What the Moon Saw*. New York: Oxford University Press, 1978.

Williams, Barbara. *Albert's Toothache,* illus. Kay Chorao. New York: E.P. Dutton and Company, 1974.

———— . *Kevin's Grandmother,* illus. Kay Chorao. New York: E.P. Dutton and Company, 1975.

Winn, Marie. *What Shall We Do and Allee Galloo!* New York: Harper and Row, 1970.

Wood, Joyce. *Grandmother Lucy Goes on a Picnic,* illus. Frank Francis. Cleveland: Collins-World Publishing Company, 1976.

Yolen, Jane. *No Bath Tonight,* illus. Nancy Winslow Parker. New York: Thomas Y. Crowell, 1978.

Young, Miriam. *If I Drove a Tractor,* illus. Robert Quackenbush. New York: Lothrop, Lee and Shephard, 1973.

Zalben, Jane Breskin. *Norton's Nightmare.* New York: Collins, 1979.

Zemach, Margot. *Hush, Little Baby.* New York: E.P. Dutton and Company, 1976.

Zolotow, Charlotte. *Hold My Hand,* illus. Thomas di Grazia. New York: Harper and Row, 1972.

————— . *May I Visit?* illus. Erik Blegvad. New York: Harper and Row, 1976.

————— . *The Unfriendly Book,* illus. William Pène du Bois. New York: Harper and Row, 1975.

Appendix B
A Selected Bibliography of Contemporary Poetry for Children

Adams, Adrienne, compil. *Poetry of Earth*. New York: Charles Scribner's Sons, 1972.

Adoff, Arnold. *make a circle keep us in*. New York: Delacorte Press, 1975.

——— . compil. *My Black Me*. New York: E. P. Dutton and Company, 1974. (Black poetry)

Aiken, Joan. *The Skin Spinners*. New York: Viking Press, 1976.

Atwood, Ann. *Haiku-Vision*. New York: Charles Scribner's Sons, 1977.

Baron, Virginia Olsen, compil. *Sunset in a Spider Web*. New York: Holt, Rinehart and Winston, 1974. (Sijo poetry, an ancient Korean form)

Belting, Natalia. *Our Fathers Had Powerful Songs*. New York: E. P. Dutton and Company, 1974. (American Indian)

Blegvad, Lenore, compil. *This Little Pig-A-Wig*. New York: Atheneum, 1978.

Bodecker, N. M. *Let's Marry, Said the Cherry*. New York: Atheneum, 1974.

Brewton, Sara, John E. Brewton, and G. Meredith Blackburn, III. *My Tang's Tungled*. New York: Thomas Y. Crowell Company, 1973. (Tongue twisters)

Causley, Charles. *Figgie Hobbin*. New York: Walker and Company, 1973.

Ciardi, John. *Fast and Slow*. Boston: Houghton Mifflin Company, 1975.

Clymer, Theodore. *Four Corners of the Sky*. Boston: Little, Brown and Company, 1975. (American Indian)

Cole, William, compil. *A Book of Animal Poems*. New York: Viking Press, 1973.

——— . *Oh, Such Foolishness!* illus. Tomie de Paola. Philadelphia: J. B. Lippincott Company, 1978.

——— . *Oh, That's Ridiculous*. New York: Viking Press, 1972.

———. *Pick Me Up*. New York: Macmillian Publishing Company, 1972.

Fisher, Aileen. *My Cat Has Eyes of Sapphire Blue*. New York: Thomas Y. Crowell Company, 1973.

Fowke, Edith. *Ring Around the Moon*. Englewood Cliffs, N.J.: Prentice-Hall, 1977. (Songs, tongue twisters, riddles, and rhymes)

Froman, Robert. *Seeing Things*. New York: Thomas Y. Crowell Company, 1974. (Concrete poetry)

Gardner, John. *A Child' Bestiary*. New York: Alfred A. Knopf, 1977.

Greenfield, Eloise. *Honey I Love,* illus. Diane and Leo Dillon. New York: Thomas Y. Crowell Company, 1978. (Black poetry)

Grimes, Nikki. *Something on My Mind,* illus. Tom Feelings. New York: Dial Press, 1978. (Black poetry)

Hoberman, Mary Ann. *Bugs*. New York: Viking Press, 1976.

——— . *The Raucous Auk*. New York: Viking Press, 1973.

Holman, Felice. *I Hear You Smiling and Other Poems*. New York: Charles Scribner's Sons, 1973.

Hood, Flora, compil. *The Turquoise Horse*. New York: Alfred A. Knopf, 1974. (Black poetry)

Hopkins, Lee Bennett, compil. *Moments*. New York: Harcourt Brace World, 1980.

Houston, James, compil. *Songs of the Dream People*. New York: Atheneum, 1972. (American Indian)

Hughes, Ted. *Season Songs*. New York: Viking Press, 1975.

Kennedy, X. J. *One Winter Night in August*. New York: Atheneum, 1972.

Kherdian, David. *Country Cat City Cat,* illus. Nonny Hogrogian. New York: Four Winds Press, 1977.

Kherdian, David, compil. *The Dog Writes on the Window With His Nose,* illus. Nonny Hogrogian. New York: Four Winds Press, 1977.

Kuskin, Karla. *Any Me I Want to Be*. New York: Harper and Row, 1972.

————— . *Near the Window Tree*. New York: Harper and Row, 1975.

Larrick, Nancy, compil. *Crazy To Be Alive*. New York: M. Evans and Company, 1977.

Lee, Dennis. *Alligator Pie*. Boston: Houghton Mifflin Company, 1975.

Livingston, Myra Cohn. *Callooh! Callay*. New York: Atheneum, 1978. (Holiday poems)

————— , compil. *Poems of Christmas*. New York: Atheneum, 1980.

————— . *The Malibu and Other Poems*. New York: Atheneum, 1972.

————— . *O Sliver of Liver*. New York: Atheneum, 1979.

————— . *4-Way Stop*. New York: Atheneum, 1976.

————— . *A Lollygag of Limericks*. New York: Atheneum, 1978.

Maestro, Betsy. *Fat Polka-Dot Cat*. New York: E.P. Dutton and Company, 1976. (Haiku)

Mayer, Mercer, compil. *A Poison Tree and Other Poems*. New York: Charles Scribner's Sons, 1977.

McCord, David. *Away and Ago*. Boston: Little, Brown and Company, 1975.

————— . *The Star in the Pail*. Boston: Little, Brown and Company, 1975.

Merriam, Eve. *The Birthday Card*. New York: Alfred A. Knopf, 1978.

————— . *Out Loud*. New York: Atheneum, 1973.

Mizumura, Kazue. *Flower Moon Snow*. New York: Thomas Y. Crowell Company, 1977. (Haiku)

Moore, Lilian, compil. *Go with the Poem*. New York: McGraw-Hill Book Company, 1979.

Moore, Lilian. *Little Raccoon and Poems From the Woods*. St. Louis: McGraw-Hill Book Company, 1975.

————— . *See My Lovely Poison Ivy*. New York: Atheneum, 1975.

Morrison, Bill. *Squeeze a Sneeze*. Boston: Houghton Mifflin Company, 1977. (Rhyming games)

Morrison, Lillian. *The Sidewalk Racer and Other Poems on Sports*. New York: Lothrop, Lee, and Shephard Company, 1977.

Morse, Flo. *How Does It Feel To Be a Tree?* New York: Parents' Magazine Press, 1976.

Ness, Evaline, compil. *Amelia Mixed the Mustard*. New York: Charles Scribner's Sons, 1975.

Peck, Robert Newton. *Bee Tree*. New York: Walker and Company, 1975.

Prelutsky, Jack. *It's Halloween.* New York: William Morrow and Company, 1977.
——— . *Nightmares.* New York: William Morrow and Company, 1976.
——— . *The Queen an Enene.* New York: William Morrow and Company, 1978.
——— . *The Snopp on the Sidewalk.* New York: William Morrow and Company, 1977.
Rimanelli, Griose, and Paul Pimsleur. *Poems Make Pictures, Pictures Make Poems,* illus. Ronni Solbert. New York: Pantheon Books, 1972. (Concrete poetry)
Roethke, Theodore. *Dirty Dinky and Other Creatures.* Garden City, N.Y.: Doubleday and Company, 1973.
Russo, Susan, compil. *The Moon's the North Wind's Cooky.* New York: Lothrop, Lee and Shephard Company, 1979.
Saunders, Dennis, compil. *Magic Lights and Streets of Shining Jet,* photo. Terry Williams. New York: William Morrow and Company, 1974.
Silverstein, Shel. *Where the Sidewalk Ends.* New York: Harper and Row, 1974.
Thurman, Judith. *Flashlight.* New York: Atheneum, 1976.
Tripp, Wallace. *A Great Big Ugly Man Came Up and Tied His Horse to Me.* Boston: Little, Brown and Company, 1973.
Wallace, Daisy, compil. *Monster Poems.* New York: Holiday House, 1976.
——— . *Witch Poems.* New York: Holiday House, 1976.
Watson, Clyde. *Catch Me and Kiss Me and Say It Again,* illus. Wendy Watson. New York: Collins Books, 1978.
Worth, Valerie. *Small Poems,* illus. Natalie Babbit. New York: Farrar, Straus and Giroux, 1972.
——— . *More Small Poems,* illus. Natalie Babbit. New York: Farrar, Straus and Giroux, 1976.
——— . *Still More Small Poems,* illus. Natalie Babbit. New York: Farrar, Straus and Giroux, 1978.
Yaroslava, compil. *I Like You.* New York: Charles Scribner's Sons, 1976.

Verse Stories

Adams, Richard, and Nicola Bayley. *The Tyger Voyage.* New York: Alfred A. Knopf, 1976.
Adoff, Arnold. *Tornado!* New York: Delacorte Press, 1977.
Belloc, Hilaire. *Hilaire Belloc's the Yak, the Python, the Frog.* New York: Parents' Magazine Press, 1975.
Belting, Natalie, *The Land of the Taffeta Dawn.* New York: E. P. Dutton and Company, 1973.
Brooks, Gwendolyn. *The Tiger Who Wore White Gloves.* Chicago: Third World Press, 1974.
Carroll, Lewis. *The Walrus and the Carpenter.* New York: Frederick Warne and Company, 1974.
Chukowsky, Kornei. *The Telephone,* adapt. William J. Smith and illus. Blair Lent. New York: Delacorte Press, 1977.
Hanlon, Emily. *How a Horse Grew Hoarse on the Site He Sighted a Bare Bear.* New York: Delacorte Press, 1976.
Paterson, A. B. *Mulga Bill's Bicycle.* New York: Parents' Magazine Press, 1973.

Appendix C
Literature, Language and Thought

Developing Powers of Observation

Anno, Mitsumasa. *Anno's Alphabet*. New York: Thomas Y. Crowell Company, 1977.

——— . *Anno's Counting Book*. New York: Thomas Y. Crowell Company, 1975.

——— . *Anno's Italy*. New York: Collins, 1978.

——— . *The King's Flower*. New York: Collins, 1978.

Aruego, Jose and Ariane Dewey. *We Hide, You Seek*. New York: William Morrow and Company, 1979.

Asch, Frank. *Moon Bear*. New York: Charles Scribner's Sons, 1978.

Brown, Marcia. *Once a Mouse*. New York: Charles Scribner's Sons, 1961.

Brown, Margaret Wise. *Fox Eyes,* illus. Garth Williams. New York: Pantheon Books, 1977.

Burton, Virginia Lee. *The Little House*. Boston: Houghton Mifflin Company, 1942.

Charlip, Remy, and Jerry Joyner. *Thirteen*. New York: Parents' Magazine Press, 1975.

Livermore, Elaine. *Lost and Found*. Boston: Houghton Mifflin Company, 1975.

Lobel, Arnold. *On Market Street,* illus. Anita Lobel. New York: Greenwillow Books, 1981.

*Press, Ham Jurgen. *The Adventures of the Black Hand Gang*. Englewood Cliffs, N.J.: Prentice-Hall, 1977.

Scheer, Julian. *Rain Makes Applesauce,* illus. Marvin Bileck. New York: Holiday House, 1964.

Sendak, Maurice. *Where the Wild Things Are*. New York: Harper and Row, 1963.

Turpin, Lorna. *The Sultan's Snakes*. New York: Greenwillow Books, 1979.

Waber, Bernard. *The Snake*. Boston: Houghton Mifflin Company, 1978.

Ward, Lynd. *The Biggest Bear*. Boston: Houghton Mifflin Company, 1952.

——— . *The Silver Pony*. Boston: Houghton Mifflin Company, 1952.

Wildsmith, Brian. *Puzzles*. London: Oxford University Press, 1970.

Yolen, Jane. *The Seeing Stick,* illus. Remy Charlip and Demetra Maraslis. New York: Thomas Y. Crowell Company, 1977.

Enjoying Repetition and Refrain

*Adkins, Jan. *Luther Tarbox*. New York: Charles Scribner's Sons, 1977.

Adoff, Arnold. *Where Wild Willie,* illus. Emily Arnold McCully. New York: Harper and Row, 1978.

Bang, Betsy. *The Old Woman and the Pumpkin,* illus. Molley Garrett. New York: Macmillan Publishing Company, 1975.

Coombs, Patricia. *The Magic Pot*. New York: Lothrop, Lee and Shephard, 1977.

Duff, Maggie. *Rum, Pum, Pum,* illus. Jose Aruego and Ariane Dewey. New York: Macmillan Publishing Company, 1978.

Charlotte Huck, The Ohio State University, provided the organizational idea for this appendix.

*Full-length book.

Gág, Wanda. *Millions of Cats.* New York: Coward, McCann and Geoghegan, 1927.

Gage, Wilson. *Down in the Boondocks,* illus. Glen Rounds. New York: William Morrow and Company, 1977.

Galdone, Joan. *The Tallypo,* illus. Paul Galdone. New York: Seabury Press, 1977.

Gauch, Patricia Lee. *On to Widecombe Fair,* illus. Trina Schart Hyman. New York: G. P. Putnam's Sons, 1978.

Horwitz, Elinor Lander. *When the Sky Is Like Lace,* illus. Barbara Cooney. Philadelphia: J.B. Lippincott Company, 1975.

Kahl, Virginia. *The Duchess Bakes a Cake.* New York: Charles Scribner's Sons, 1955.

Platz, Nancy. *Pumpernickel Tickle and Mean Green Cheese.* New York: Franklin Watts, 1978.

Prelutsky, Jack. *The Mean Old Mean Hyena,* illus. Arnold Lobel. New York: William Morrow and Company, 1978.

Pomerantz, Charlotte. *The Mango Tooth.* New York: William Morrow and Company, 1977.

Sendak, Maurice. *Chicken Soup With Rice.* New York: Harper and Row, 1962.

Stern, Simon. *The Hobyahs.* Englewood Cliffs, N.J.: Prentice-Hall, 1977.

Westerberg, Christine. *The Cap That Mother Made.* New York: Prentice-Hall, 1977.

Recognizing Patterns of Plot Structures

Patterns of Three

Many folk tales

Berson, Harold. *Joseph and the Snake.* New York: Macmillan Publishing Company, 1979.

Lobel, Arnold. *A Treeful of Pigs,* illus. Anita Lobel. New York: William Morrow and Company, 1979.

Surprise Endings

Allen, Linda. *Lionel and the Spy Next Door.* New York: William Morrow and Company, 1980.

*Heide, Florence Parry. *Banana Twist.* New York: Holiday House, 1978.

Mayer, Mercer, *Bubble Bubble.* New York: Parents' Magazine Press, 1973.

Parker, Nancy Winslow. *The Crocodile Under Louis Finneberg's Bed.* New York: Dodd, Mead and Company, 1978.

Pomerantz, Charlotte. *The Mango Tooth.* New York: William Morrow and Company, 1977.

Raskin, Ellen. *Moose Goose and Little Nobody.* New York: Parents' Magazine Press, 1974.

Ruffins, Reynold. *My Brother Never Feeds the Cat.* New York: Charles Scribner's Sons, 1979.

Wells, Rosemary. *Abdul.* New York: Dial Press, 1975.

———— . *Unfortunately Harriet.* New York: Dial Press, 1972.

Williams, Barbara. *Albert's Toothache,* illus. Kay Chorao. New York: E. P. Dutton and Company, 1974.

*Full-length book.

Yolen, Jane. *The Seeing Stick,* illus. Remy Charlip and Demetra Maraslis. New York: Thomas Y. Crowell Company, 1977.

Zolotow, Charlotte. *The Unfriendly Book,* illus. William Pène Du Bois. New York: Harper and Row, 1975.

Cumulative Tales

Aardema, Verna. *Bringing the Rain to Kapiti Plain,* illus, Beatriz Vidal. New York: Dial Press, 1981.

Bonne, Rose. *I Know an Old Lady,* illus. Abner Graboff. New York: Rand McNally and Company, 1961.

Brown, Marcia. *The Bun.* New York: Harcourt Brace Jovanovich, 1972.

Burningham, John. *The Shopping Basket.* New York: Thomas Y. Crowell, 1980.

———— . *Time To Get Out of the Bath.* New York: Thomas Y. Crowell Company, 1978.

Flack, Marjorie. *Ask Mr. Bear.* New York: Macmillan Publishing Company, 1932.

Frasconi, Antonio. *The House That Jack Built.* New York: Harcourt Brace Jovanovich, 1958.

Garrison, Christian. *Little Pieces of the West Wind,* illus. Diane Goode. Scarsdale, N.Y.: Seabury Press, 1975.

Hogrogian, Nonny. *One Fine Day.* New York: Macmillan Publishing Company, 1975.

Kuskin, Karla. *A Boy Had a Mother Who Bought Him a Hat.* Boston: Houghton Mifflin Company, 1976.

Lobel, Anita. *King Rooster, Queen Hen.* New York: William Morrow Company, 1975.

Rockwell, Anne. *Poor Goose.* New York: Thomas Y. Crowell Company, 1976.

Zemach, Margot. *It Could Always Be Worse.* New York: Farrar, Straus and Giroux, 1976.

Zolotow, Charlotte, *Mr. Rabbit and the Lovely Present,* illus. Maurice Sendak. New York: Harper and Row, 1962.

Full Circle

Brown, Marcia. *Once a Mouse.* New York: Charles Scribner's Sons, 1961.

Hoffman, Felix. *Hans in Luck.* New York: Atheneum, 1975.

McDermott, Gerald. *Anansi and the Spider.* New York: Holt, Rinehart and Winston, 1972.

———— . *The Stonecutter.* New York: Viking Press, 1975.

Zemach, Kaethe. *The Beautiful Rat.* New York: Four Winds Press, 1979.

Parallel Plot

Burningham, John. *Come Away From the Water, Shirley.* New York: Thomas Y. Crowell, Company, 1977.

*Konigsburg, E. L. *Father's Arcane Daughter.* New York: Atheneum, 1976.

McCloskey, Robert. *Blueberries for Sal.* New York: Viking Press, 1948.

McLeod, Emilie Warren. *The Bear's Bicycle.* Boston: Little, Brown and Company, 1975.

*Orgel, Doris. *A Certain Magic.* New York: Dial Press, 1976.

*Full-length book.

Schweitzer, Byrd Baylor. *Amigo,* illus. Garth Williams. New York: Collier and World Publishing Company, 1963.

Shector, Ben. *Conrad's Castle.* New York: Harper and Row, 1967.

Cause and Effect

Aardema, Verna. *Why Mosquitoes Buzz in People's Ears,* illus. Leo and Diane Dillon. New York: Dial Press, 1975.

Barton, Byron. *Buzz Buzz Buzz.* New York: Macmillan Publishing Company, 1973.

Identifying Point of View—Illustrations and Content

Adler, David A. *You Think It's Fun to be a Clown,* illus. Ray Cruz. Garden City, N.Y.: Doubleday and Company, 1980.

*Arthur, Ruth M. *An Old Magic.* New York: Atheneum, 1977.

*Avi. *A Place Called Ugly.* New York: Pantheon Books, 1981.

*Buchwald, Emilie. *Gildaen.* New York: Harcourt Brace Jovanovich, 1973.

*Burchard, Peter. *Digger.* New York: G. P. Putnam's Sons, 1980.

Fatio, Louise. *The Happy Lion,* illus. Roger Duvoisin. New York: McGraw-Hill, 1954.

*Gripe, Julia. *Julia's House.* New York: Delacorte Press, 1971.

*Härtling, Peter. *Oma.* New York: Delacorte Press, 1971.

*Hickman, Janet. *The Stones.* New York: Macmillan, 1976.

*Lively, Penelope. *Fanny's Sister.* New York: E. P. Dutton, 1976.

Raskin, Ellen. *Nothing Ever Happens on My Block.* New York: Atheneum, 1968.

*Rodgers, Mary. *Freaky Friday.* New York: Harper and Row, 1972.

*St. George, Judith. *The Halo Wind.* New York: G. P. Putnam's Sons, 1978.

Sharmat, Marjorie. *Gila Monsters Meet You at the Airport,* illus. Bryon Barton. New York: Macmillan Publishing Company, 1980.

Sharmat, Marjorie, and Mitchell Sharmat. *I Am Not a Pest,* illus. Diane Dawson. New York: E. P. Dutton and Company, 1979.

———— . *The Day I Was Born,* illus. Diane Dawson. New York: E. P. Dutton, 1980.

Tresselt, Alvin. *Hide and Seek Fog,* illus. Roger Duvoisin. New York: Lothrop, Lee and Shephard, 1965.

Waber, Bernard. *You're a Little Kid with a Big Heart.* Boston: Houghton Mifflin Company, 1980.

Williams, Jay. *The City Witch and the Country Witch,* illus. Ed Renfro. New York: Macmillan Publishing Company, 1979.

*Young, Alida E. *Land of the Iron Dragon.* Garden City, N.Y.: Doubleday and Company, 1978.

Zemach, Margot. *To Hilda for Helping.* New York: Farrar, Straus and Giroux, 1977.

*Full-length book.

Appreciating Imagery

Adoff, Arnold. *Under the Morning Trees,* illus. Ronald Himler. New York: E. P. Dutton and Company, 1978.

Baylor, Byrd. *Guess Who My Favorite Person Is,* illus. Robert Andrew Parker. New York: Charles Scribner's Sons, 1977.

Baylor, Byrd, and Peter Parnall. *The Other Way To Listen.* New York: Charles Scribner's Sons, 1978.

Brown, Marcia. *Listen to a Shape.* New York: Franklin Watts, 1979.

————. *Touch Will Tell.* New York: Franklin Watts, 1979.

————. *Walk With Your Eyes.* New York: Franklin Watts, 1979.

Garelick, May. *Down to the Beach,* illus. Barbara Cooney. New York: Four Winds Press, 1973.

Horwitz, Elinor Lander. *When the Sky Is Like Lace,* illus. Barbara Cooney. Philadelphia: J. B. Lippincott Company, 1975.

Hurd, Thacher. *The Quiet Evening.* New York: William Morrow and Company, 1978.

Jensen, Virginia Allen and Polly Edman. *Red Thread Riddles.* New York: Collins, 1979.

Lionni, Leo. *Frederick.* New York: Pantheon Books, 1967.

————. *Swimmy.* New York: Pantheon Books, 1963.

Lund, Doris Herald. *The Paint-Box Sea,* illus. Symeon Shimin. New York: McGraw-Hill Book Company, 1973.

Mac Lachlan, Patricia. *Through Grandpa's Eyes,* illus. Deborah Ray. New York: Harper and Row, 1979.

O'Neil, Mary. *Hailstones and Halibut Bones.* Garden City, N.Y.: Doubleday and Company, 1961.

Tresselt, Alvin. *Hide and Seek Fog,* illus. Roger Duvoisin. New York: Lothrop, Lee and Shephard, 1965.

————. *White Snow, Bright Snow,* illus. Roger Duvoisin. New York: Lothrop, Lee and Shephard, 1947.

————. *What Did You Leave Behind?* illus. Roger Duvoisin. New York: Lothrop, Lee and Shephard, 1978.

Tudor, Tasha. *Tasha Tudor's Five Senses.* New York: Platt and Munk, 1978.

Yolen, Jane. *The Seeing Stick,* illus. Remy Charlip and Demetra Maraslis. New York: Thomas Y. Crowell Company, 1977.

Concept Books To Extend Imagery

Hatch, Shirley Cook. *Wind Is To Feel.* New York: Coward, McCann and Geoghegan, 1973.

Price, Christine. *Talking Drums of Africa.* New York: Charles Scribner's Sons, 1973.

Yolen, Jane. *Ring Out!* New York: Seabury Press, 1974.

Book Containing Sensory Experiences

Kohl, Judith, and Herbert Kohl. *The View From the Oak.* New York: Charles Scribner's Sons, 1977.

Appreciating Figurative Language

*Calvert, Patricia. *The Snowbird*. New York: Charles Scribner's Sons, 1980.

Chaffin, Lillie D. *We Be Warm Till Springtime Comes,* illus. Lloyd Bloom. New York: Macmillan Publishing Company, 1980.

Farber, Norma. *There Once Was a Woman Who Married a Man,* illus. Ludia Dabcovich. Reading, Mass.: Addison-Wesley, 1968.

Hann, Jacquie. *Crybaby*. New York: Four Winds Press, 1979.

*Keith, Harold. *The Obstinate Land*. New York: Thomas Y. Crowell Company, 1977.

Lionni, Leo. *Swimmy*. New York: Pantheon Books, 1963.

Lund, Doris Herald. *The Paint-Box Sea,* illus. Symeon Shimin. New York: McGraw-Hill Book Company, 1973.

McCloskey, Robert. *Time of Wonder*. New York: Viking Press, 1957.

*Paterson, Katherine. *The Great Gilly Hopkins*. New York: Thomas Y. Crowell Company, 1978.

Tresselt, Alvin. *A Thousand Lights and Fireflies,* illus. John Moodie. New York: Parents' Magazine Press, 1965.

————— . *White Snow, Bright Snow,* illus. Roger Duvoisin. New York: Lothrop, Lee and Shephard, 1947.

Comparing and Contrasting Themes and Different Versions

Themes

"Wishing To Be Somebody Else"

Bailey, Carolyn S. *The Little Rabbit Who Wanted Red Wings*. New York: Platt and Munk, 1931.

Freeman, Don. *Dandelion*. New York: Viking Press, 1964.

Waber, Bernard. *You Look Ridiculous*. Boston: Houghton Mifflin Company, 1966.

Zion, Gene. *Harry the Dirty Dog,* illus. Margaret Bloy Graham. New York: Harper and Row, 1969.

"Assuming Superior Traits"

Duvoisin, Roger. *Petunia*. New York: Alfred A. Knopf, 1950.

Massie, Diane. *Dazzle*. New York: Parents' Magazine Press, 1969.

"Everyone Has Something To Offer"

Peet, Bill. *The Spooky Tail of Prewitt Peacock*. Boston: Houghton Mifflin Company, 1972.

Wildsmith, Brian. *The Little Wood Duck*. New York: Franklin Watts, 1973.

"Resentment of New Sibling"

Hoban, Russell. *A Baby Sister for Frances,* illus. Lillian Hoban. New York: Harper and Row, 1964.

Keats, Ezra Jack. *Peter's Chair*. New York: Harper and Row, 1967.

Scott, Ann Herbert. *On Mother's Lap*. New York: McGraw-Hill Book Company, 1972.

Wells, Rosemary. *Noisy Nora*. New York: Dial Press, 1973.

*Full-length book.

Different Versions

Brown, Marcia. *Stone Soup*. New York: Charles Scribner's Sons, 1947.

Zemach, Harve. *Nail Soup,* illus. Margot Zemach. Chicago: Follett Publishing Company, 1964.

Rumpelstiltskin

Ness, Evaline. *Tom Tit Tot*. New York: Charles Scribner's Sons, 1965.

Zemach, Harve, and Margot Zemach. *Duffy and the Devil*. New York: Farrar, Straus and Giroux, 1973.

The Little Red Hen

Domanska, Janina. *Little Red Hen*. New York: Macmillan Publishing Company, 1973.

Galdone, Paul. *The Little Red Hen*. New York: Seabury Press, 1973.

Little Red Riding Hood

de Regniers, Beatrice Schenk. *Red Riding Hood*. New York: Atheneum, 1972.

Galdone, Paul. *Little Red Riding Hood*. New York: McGraw-Hill Publishing Company, 1974.

Cinderella

Clark, Ann Nolan. *In the Land of Small Dragon,* illus. Tony Chen. New York: Viking Press, 1979.

Galdone, Paul. *Cinderella*. New York: McGraw-Hill Publishing Company, 1978.

Grimm. *Cinderella,* illus. Svend Otto S. New York: Larousse and Company, 1978.

Hogrogian, Nonny. *Cinderella*. New York: Greenwillow Books, 1981.

*Murphy, Shirley Rousseau. *Silver Woven in My Hair*. New York: Atheneum, 1977.

Discovering Theme and Layers of Meaning

Brown, Marcia. *Once a Mouse*. New York: Charles Scribner's Sons, 1961.

Freeman, Don. *Dandelion*. New York: Viking Press, 1964.

Lionni, Leo. *Frederick*. New York: Pantheon Books, 1967.

———. *Swimmy*. New York: Pantheon Books, 1963.

Parker, Nancy Winslow. *The Crocodile Under Louis Finneberg's Bed*. New York: Dodd, Mead and Company, 1978.

Shector, Ben. *Conrad's Castle*. New York: Harper and Row, 1979.

*White, E. B. *Charlotte's Web,* illus. Garth Williams. New York: Harper and Row, 1952.

Yashima, Taro. *Crow Boy*. New York: Viking Press, 1955.

Understanding Symbolism—Illustrations and Content

*Cunningham, Julia. *Come to the Edge*. New York: Pantheon Books, 1977.

*———. *Tuppeny*. New York: E. P. Dutton and Company, 1978.

Rosen, Winifred. *Dragons Hate To Be Discreet,* illus. Edward Koren. New York: Alfred A. Knopf, 1978.

*Full-length book.

Sendak, Maurice. *Where the Wild Things Are*. New York: Harper and Row, 1963.

Shector, Ben. *Conrad's Castle*. New York: Harper and Row, 1967.

*Sperry, Armstrong. *Call It Courage*. New York: Macmillan Publishing Company, 1940.

Ward, Lynd. *The Silver Pony*. Boston: Houghton Mifflin Company, 1973.

Yashima, Taro. *Crow Boy*. New York: Viking Press, 1955.

*Full-length book.

Appendix D
Sources of Media for Children's Literature

American Library Association
   35 W. 4th Street
   New York, NY 10036

Caedmon Records
   505 8th Avenue
   New York, NY 10018

CCM Films (Crowell-Collier-Macmillan School and Library Services)
   110 15th Street
   Del-Mar, CA 92014

Children's Book Council
   67 Irving Place
   New York, NY 10003

Encyclopedia Britannica
   Educational Corporation
   425 N. Michigan Avenue
   Chicago, IL 60611

Folkways/Scholastic
   906 Sylvan Avenue
   Englewood Cliffs, NJ 07632

London Records
   539 W. 25th Street
   New York, NY 10001

McGraw-Hill Films
   1221 Avenue of the Americas
   New York, NY 10020

Miller-Brody
   342 Madison Avenue
   New York, NY 10017

National Film Board of Canada
   1350 Avenue of the Americas
   New York, NY 10020

Newbery Awards Records
   342 Madison Avenue
   New York, NY 10017

Scholastic Magazines
   904 Sylvan Avenue
   Englewood Cliffs, NJ 07632

SVE (Society for Visual Education)
   1345 Diversey Parkway
   Chicago, IL 60614

Viking Press
   625 Madison Avenue
   New York, NY 10022

Weston Woods Studios
   Weston, CT 06880

Appendix E
A Selected Bibliography of
Literature and Music

Aliki. *Go Tell Aunt Rhody.* New York: Macmillan Publishing Company, 1974.

Bryan, Ashley. *Walk Together Children.* New York: Atheneum, 1974. (Black American Spirituals)

Conover, Chris. *Six Little Ducks.* New York: Thomas Y. Crowell Company, 1976.

Gage, Wilson. *Down in the Boondocks,* illus. Glen Rounds. New York: William Morrow and Company, 1977. (Creative Activity)

Gauch, Patricia Lee. *On the Widecombe Fair,* illus. Trina Schart Hyman. New York: G.P. Putnam's Sons, 1978.

Gerson, Mary Joan. *Omoteji's Baby Brother,* illus. Elizia Moon. New York: Henry Z. Walck, 1974. (Music and Movement)

Hazen, Barbara Shook. *Where Do Bears Sleep?,* illus. Ian E. Staunton. Reading, Mass.: Addison-Wesley, 1970. (Lullaby)

Hoban, Russell. *Bread and Jam,* illus. Lillian Hoban. New York: Harper and Row, 1964.

————— . Egg *Thoughts and Other Frances Songs,* illus. Lillian Hoban. New York: Harper and Row, 1972.

Hoffman, Hilde. *The Green Grass Grows All Around.* New York: Macmillan Publishing Company, 1968.

Horwitz, Elinor Lander. *When the Sky is Like Lace,* illus. Barbara Cooney. Philadelphia: J.B. Lippincott Company, 1975.

Leodhas, Sorche Nic. *Always Room For One More,* illus. Nonny Hogrogian. New York: Holt, Rinehart and Winston, 1965.

Longstaff, John. *Hot Cross Buns and Other Old Street Cries.* New York: Atheneum, 1977.

————— . *Sweetly Sings the Donkey,* illus. Nancy Winslow Parker. New York: Atheneum, 1976. (Rounds)

Marzollo, Jean. *Close Your Eyes,* illus. Susan Jeffers. New York: Dial Press, 1978.

Nelson, Esther L. *Movement Games.* New York: Sterling Publishing Company, 1975.

Prokofiev, Sergei. *Peter and the Wolf,* illus. Erna Voight. Boston: David R. Godine, 1979.

Quackenbush, Robert. *Pop! Goes the Weasel and Yankee Doodle.* Philadelphia: J.B. Lippincott Company, 1976.

Yolen, Jane. *All in the Woodland Early,* illus. Jane Breskin Zalben. New York: Collins, 1979.

————— . *Rounds About Rounds.* New York: Franklin Watts, 1977.

Zemach, Margot. *Hush, Little Baby.* New York: E.P. Dutton and Company, 1976.

Appendix F
Literature and Flannelboard Stories*

Aardema, Verna. *Why Mosquitoes Buzz in People's Ears,* illus. Leo and Diane Dillon. New York: Dial Press, 1975.

Asch, Frank. *Turtle Tree.* New York: Dial Press, 1978.

Bailey, Carolyn Sherwin. *The Little Rabbit Who Wanted Red Wings.* New York: Platt and Munk, 1931.

Berson, Joseph. *Joseph and the Snake.* New York: Macmillan Publishing Company, 1979.

Brown, Marcia. *The Bun.* New York: Harcourt Brace Jovanovich, 1972.

———. *Once a Mouse.* New York: Charles Scribner's Sons, 1961.

Burningham, John. *Mr. Gumpy's Outing.* New York: Holt, Rinehart and Winston, 1971.

Carle, Eric. *A Very Hungry Caterpillar.* New York: World Publishing Company, n.d.

Gackenbush, Dick. *Hattie Rabbit.* New York: Harper and Row, 1976.

Ginsburg, Mirra. *The Strongest One of All,* illus. Jose Aruego and Ariane Dewey. New York: William Morrow and Company, 1977.

———. *Where Does the Sun Go at Night?* illus. Jose Aruego and Ariane Dewey. New York: Greenwillow Books, 1981.

Hoffman, Felix. *Hans in Luck.* New York: Atheneum, 1975.

Hogrogian, Nonny. *One Fine Day.* New York: Collier Books, 1971.

Jeschke, Susan. *Sidney.* New York: Henry Z. Walck, 1975.

Keats, Ezra Jack. *Over in the Meadow.* New York: Four Winds Press, 1972.

Lobel, Anita. *King Rooster, Queen Hen.* New York: William Morrow and Company, 1975.

Maitland, Anthony. *Idle Jack.* New York: Farrar, Straus and Giroux, 1977.

Massie, Diane Redfield. *Dazzle.* New York: Parents' Magazine Press, 1969.

McDermott, Gerald. *The Stonecutter.* New York: Viking Press, 1975.

McPhail, David. *Grandfather's Cake.* New York: Charles Scribner's Sons, 1979.

Miles, Miska. *Chicken Forgets.* Boston: Little, Brown and Company, 1976.

———. *Swim, Little Duck,* illus. Jim Arnosky. Boston: Little, Brown and Company, 1976.

Preston, Edna Mitchell. *Squawk to the Moon, Little Goose,* illus. Barbara Cooney. New York: Viking Press, 1974.

Sendak, Maurice. *Where the Wild Things Are.* New York: Harper and Row, 1963.

Steig, William. *The Amazing Bone.* New York: Farrar, Straus and Giroux, 1976.

———. *Sylvester and the Magic Pebble.* New York: Windmill Books, 1969.

Zemach, Kaethe. *The Beautiful Rat.* New York: Four Winds Press, 1979.

*Many of the simple folktales make good flannelboard presentations.

Appendix G
Literature and Narrative Pantomime

Picture Books

Barton, Byron. *Buzz Buzz Buzz*. New York: Macmillan Publishing Company, 1973.

Daughtery, James. *Andy and the Lion*. New York: Viking Press, 1966.

de Regniers, Beatrice Schenk. *Red Riding Hood*. New York: Atheneum, 1972.

Freeman, Don. *Beady Bear*. New York: Viking Press, 1954.

Galdone, Paul. *The History of Mother Twaddle and the Marvelous Achievements of Her Son Jack*. New York: Seabury Press, 1974.

Hoban, Russell. *How Tom Beat Captain Najork and His Hired Sportsmen,* illus. Quentin Blake. New York: Atheneum, 1974.

Hoffmann, Felix. *Hans in Luck*. New York: Atheneum, 1975.

Johnson, Crockett. *Harold and the Purple Crayon*. New York: Harper and Row, 1955.

Joslin, Sesyle. *What Do You Do, Dear?* illus. Maurice Sendak. New York: W. R. Scott, 1961.

Keats, Ezra Jack. *The Snowy Day*. New York: Viking Press, 1962.

Kuratomi, Chizuko. *Mr. Bear and the Robbers,* illus. Kozo Kakimoto. New York: Dial Press, 1970.

Lobel, Arnold. *How the Rooster Saved the Day,* illus. Anita Lobel. New York: William Morrow and Company, 1977.

———— . *The Man Who Took the Indoors Out*. New York: Harper and Row, 1974.

Montresor, Beni. *Bedtime!* New York: Harper and Row, 1978.

Paterson, Diane. *If I Were a Toad*. New York: Dial Press, 1977.

Preston, Edna Mitchell. *Squawk to the Moon, Little Goose*. New York: Viking Press, 1974.

Ryan, Cheli Duran. *Hildilid's Night,* illus. Arnold Lobel. New York: Macmillan Publishing Company, 1971.

Tolstoy, Alexei. *The Great Big Enormous Turnip*. New York: Franklin Watts, 1968.

Wells, Rosemary. *Unfortunately Harriet*. New York: Dial Press, 1972.

Poems

Greenfield, Eloise. *Honey, I Love,* illus. Diane and Leo Dillon. New York: Thomas Y. Crowell Company, 1978.
"Rope Rhyme"

Holman, Felice. *At the Top of My Voice,* illus. Edward Gorey. New York: Charles Scribner's Sons, 1970.
"I Can Fly"
"Wild Day at the Shore"

Livingston, Myra Cohn. *4-Way Stop*. New York: Atheneum, 1976.
    "Bubble Gum"
    "The Biggest Laugh"
McCord, David. *Every Time I Climb a Tree,* illus. Marc Simont. Boston: Little, Brown, and Company, 1967.
    "The Pickety Fence"
    "Pad and Pencil"
Merriman, Eve. *Out Loud*. New York: Atheneum, 1973.
    "Windshield Wiper"
Morrison, Lillian. *The Sidewalk Racer and Other Poems on Sports and Motion.* New York: Lothrop, Lee and Shephard, 1977.
    "Forms of Praise"
    "The Sidewalk Racer"
    "I Love All Gravity Defiers"
    "The Surfer"
    "The Angels of Motion"
    "Nine Triads"
Thurman, Judith. *Flashlight*. New York: Atheneum, 1976.
    "Flashlight"
    "Balloon!"
    "Playing Clay"

Appendix H
Poetry Forms

Short-Verse Forms

Haiku

Origin: Japan

Characteristics: Captures a moment in the world of nature or in a season of the year.

Form:

    17 syllables

Line 1	5 syllables
Line 2	7 syllables
Line 3	5 syllables

References:

Atwood, Ann. *Haiku—Vision.* New York: Charles Scribner's Sons, 1977.

Behn, Harry, trans. *Cricket Songs.* New York: Harcourt, Brace and World, 1964.

Caudill, Rebecca. *Come Along.* New York: Holt, Rinehart and Winston, 1969.

Lewis, Richard, ed. *In a Spring Garden,* illus. Ezra Jack Keats. New York: Dial Press, 1965.

Mizumura, Kazue. *Flower Snow Moon.* New York: Thomas Y. Crowell Company, 1977.

Senryu

Origin: Japan

Characteristics:

1. Concentrates on a single idea or image of a moment
2. Relates to any idea or subject

Form:

    17 syllables

Line 1	5 syllables
Line 2	7 syllables
Line 3	5 syllables

Tanka

Origin: Japan

Characteristics: Deals with nature or a season of the year

Form:

31 syllables

Line 1	5 syllables
Line 2	7 syllables
Line 3	5 syllables
Line 4	7 syllables
Line 5	7 syllables

References:

Baron, Virginia Olsen, compil. *The Seasons of Time: Poetry of Ancient Japan.* New York: Dial Press, 1968.

Sijo (she—jo)

Origin: Korea

Characteristics:

1. Usually deals with nature or a season
2. Is similar to haiku; based on syllabification and unrhymed

Form:

1. 6 lines
2. each line containing 7 or 8 syllables
3. total syllables: 42 to 48

References:

Baron, Virginia Olsen, compil. *Sunset in a Spider's Web.* New York: Holt, Rinehart and Winston, 1974.

Hopkins, Lee Bennett. "Sijo." *The Instructor,* March, 1969, pp. 76–77.

Lee, Peter H., trans. *Anthology of Korean Poetry.* New York: John Day Company, 1964.

——— . *Korean Literature: Themes and Topics.* Eugene, Ore.: University of Oregon Press, 1965.

Cinquain

Origin: United States

Characteristics: A story about a word

Form: (several forms)

Line 1	1 word
Line 2	2 words
Line 3	3 words
Line 4	4 words
Line 5	1 word (a synonym or summarizing word)

Examples:

Flesh
Soft rain
Taps my windowpane
Calling, "Join me outside,
Now!"
—UNI student in TELA

Snow
Whirled about
By the wind
It's very strong today!
Brr!
—UNI student in TELA

Diamante (dee—ah—mahn—tay)

Origin: United States

Characteristics: Involves a contrasting of ideas

Form: Line 1   1 word
       Line 2   2 words
       Line 3   3 words
       Line 4   4 words—transition of ideas
       Line 5   3 words
       Line 6   2 words
       Line 7   1 word—opposite of the word in Line 1

References:

Tiedt, Iris M. "A New Poetic Form: The Diamante." *Elementary English,* May, 1969, pp. 588–89.

Example:

fast
spinning, twirling
wooden horses galloping
carrousel begins to fade and die
steeds drifting along
meandering, pausing
slow
—Judy Ricca, UNI graduate student in TELA

Traditional Verse Forms

Couplet

Characteristics: Simplest form of poetry
Form: Two lines bound together by rhyme
Examples:

> Tommy's tears and Mary's fears
> Will make them old before their years.
> > —Mother Goose

> January brings the snow
> Makes our feet and fingers glow.
> > —Mother Goose

References: Many Mother Goose rhymes

> Bodecker, N. M. *It's Raining, Said John Twaining*. New York: Atheneum Press, 1973.
> Zolotow, Charlotte. *Some Things Go Together*. New York: Abelard-Schuman, 1969.

Quatrain

Form:

> 4 lines with any metrical pattern of rhyme

Limericks

(Perfected by Edward Lear)

Form: 5 lines

1. Rhyme scheme
   Lines 1, 2, and 5 rhyme.
   Lines 3 and 4 may not rhyme.

2. Meter organization
   Lines 1, 2, and 5
   -1   --1   --1
   iambus anapest anapest
   Lines 3 and 4
   --1   --1
   anapest anapest

References:

> Brewton, Sara, and John E., comp. *Laughable Limericks*. New York: Thomas Y. Crowell Company, 1965.
> Smith, William Jay. *Typewriter Town*. New York: E.P. Dutton, 1960.

Parodies

To introduce parodies, Mother Goose rhymes can be adapted.

Reference:

Livingston, Myra Cohn, compil. *Speak Roughly to Your Little Boy: A Collection of Parodies and Burlesques Together With Original Poems Chosen and Annotated for Young People.* New York: Harcourt, Brace and Jovanovich, 1971.

Experimental Verse Forms

Concrete Poetry

Characteristics: Combination of sight and sound, visual and verbal (Other senses can also be incorporated into the work.)

References:

Froman, Robert. *Seeing Things.* New York: Thomas Y. Crowell Company, 1974.

Pilon, Barbara, compil. *Concrete Is Not Always Hard.* Middletown, Conn.: Xerox Education Publications, 1972.

Rimandelli, Griose, and Paul Pinsleur. *Poems Make Pictures Pictures Make Poems,* illus. Ronni Solbert. New York: Pantheon Books, 1972.

Found Poetry

Characteristics: Phrases and sentences that appear in media—advertising phrases and slo-gans, headlines, titles, and captions, arranged in an interesting manner.

Septalet

Characteristics: A break in thought and form patterns; cause-and-effect relationship

Form:
1. 7 lines with 14 words
2. 4 lines, break in pattern, 3 lines

Example:

Snowman
round figure
broom in hand
coal eyes

Sun
shines brightly
melts my friend
—UNI student in TELA

Quinzaine

Characteristics: A statement followed by a question

Form:

    15 syllables
     3 lines
        7 syllables
        5 syllables
        3 syllables

Quintain

Origin: United States

Form: Word or syllable progress (5 lines—2, 4, 6, 8, 10)

Clerihewi

Characteristics: Two couplets

Form: Line 1   A person's name
     Line 2, 3, 4   Say something about the person

Septone

Characteristics: Seven lines (syllables or words) based on your telephone number

Form: Telephone number 351–4278

Line 1	3 syllables or words
Line 2	5 syllables or words
Line 3	1 syllable or word
Line 4	4 syllables or words
Line 5	2 syllables or words
Line 6	7 syllables or words
Line 7	8 syllables or words

Who, What, Where, When, Why

Form:

Line 1	Who
Line 2	What
Line 3	Where
Line 4	When
Line 5	Why

Examples:

Snow
falls in whispers
on the trees
during a moonlit night
so as not to disturb the life below.
—Jolene Hanig, UNI student in TELA

Pyramid Poetry

Form:

Line 1	1 word
Line 2	2 words
Line 3	3 words
Line 4	4 words

Lines 2, 3 and 4 elaborate on the word in Line 1

Combinations of Forms

Haikon

Characteristics: A combination of haiku and concrete poetry; haiku written around a picture which describes a poem

Other combinations:
Cinquain—Concrete Poetry
Diamante—Concrete Poetry

References on poetry composition for children:

Hopkins, Lee Bennett. *Pass the Poetry Please.* New York: Citation Press, 1972.

Livington, Myra Cohn. *When You Are Alone/It Keeps You Capone.* New York: Atheneum, 1973.

Tiedt, Iris M., and Sidney W. Tiedt. *Contemporary English in the Elementary School.* (2d ed.) Englewood Cliffs, N.J.: Prentice-Hall, 1975.

Appendix I
Independent Learning Centers

Literature, Language, and Other Expressive Arts

LITERATURE—Art

1. Examine Burningham's wall friezes. Compare his style in the wall friezes with his style in the illustrations in the books *Mr. Gumpy's Outing* and *Would You Rather. . . .*
2. Make a wall frieze. Suggestions:

   A lion frieze
   > Look at lion books: Fatio's *The Happy Lion,* Freeman's *Dandelion,* Daughtery's *Andy and the Lion*

   A *Swimmy* or *Frederick* frieze
   > Look at Lionni's *Swimmy* or *Frederick*

   A collage frieze
   > Look at Keat's *The Snowy Day* and *Whistle for Willie*

LITERATURE—Music, Art, and Language

1. Read Prokofieff's *Peter and the Wolf.*
2. You might like to listen to the recording of Peter and the Wolf by the London Symphony Orchestra.
3. The illustrations in the book are scratchboard. Perhaps you would like to make your own scratchboard pictures.
4. You could retell the story by placing flannelboard characters on the flannelboard while you listen to the record.

LITERATURE—Oral Language

1. Read Pat Hutchins' *Rosie's Walk.* Retell the story from the fox's point of view. Supply sound effects. Tape your story.
2. Read Maggie Duff's *Rum Pum Pum.* Retell the story using sound effects.
3. Retell the story of *The Three Bears* from different points of view: as Little Bear would have told it in sharing time; as Goldilocks would have told it to her mother; as Mother Bear would have told it in a telephone conversation with her mother-in-law; and as Father Bear would have told it at work.

LITERATURE—Rhythm

1. Read Arnold Adoff's *Ma nDa La.*
2. Explore the rhythm of *Ma nDa La.*

LITERATURE—Creative Language

1. Read books of haiku (Examples—*Haiku-Vision*, by Atwood; *Cricket Songs*, by Behn; *In a Spring Garden*, by Lewis; *Flower Moon Snow*, by Mizumura).
2. Tape or write some haiku. (You might want to find pictures on which to write haiku.)
3. Begin a book of haiku. Perhaps some of your classmates could help you. Directions for haiku:

    Content—

    A season and/or nature
    One moment in time.

    Form—three lines
    5 syllables
    7 syllables
    5 syllables

LITERATURE—Creative Language

1. Read the folders of cinquain.
2. Tape or write your own cinquains. Start with
    Words you like
    Favorite people or things
    Words about an event, a holiday, a season
3. Begin a book of cinquain.
    Some of your classmates might help you.

    Directions for cinquain:
    Line 1   one word
    Line 2   two words about the word in the first line
    Line 3   three words about the word in the first line
    Line 4   four words about the word in the first line
    Line 5   one word which summarizes the poem or is a synonym for the word in the first line

LITERATURE—Creative Language

1. Read Ciardi's *I Met A Man*. Compose riddles either in oral or written form. You may want to make a booklet. Maybe you will want to share your work with others and compile a book.
2. Read Charlip's *Fortunately*. Make up a "fortunately-unfortunately" story. Tape or write it. You might want to make a book.
3. Read *Someday*, by Charlotte Zolotow. Tell or write about your wishes. Read *Harold and the Purple Crayon*, by Crockett Johnson. Make a tape or a book telling about what you did with a crayon.
4. Read Burningham's *Would You Rather. . . .* Make a tape or write a story telling what "you would rather."

LITERATURE—Language and Art

1. Read Mary O'Neill's *Hailstones and Halibut Bones*. Each poem in her book explores experiences with a color.
2. Select a color. Tell or write about your experiences with that color.
3. You might make a collage or display relating the sensory experiences found in a color.

LITERATURE—Written Language and Art

1. Make a thumbprint book. (See Krauss' *This Thumbprint*.).
2. Make an impressionalist art book. (See *Little Red Riding Hood*, printed by Museum of Modern Art.)
3. Make a book of cinquain or haiku. (See the center on poetry forms.)
4. Experiment with gum eraser printing. Look at Keat's *The Snowy Day*. You might want to use gum eraser printing to illustrate the end papers of your book.
5. Make a word book. (See Mary O'Neill's *Words, Words, Words*.)
   Things to put in your word book—list words and/or write stories about the words you especially like:
   > Words which make you laugh
   > Words which sound like their names
   > Words for loud sounds
   > Words which mean love
   > Mysterious words
   > Words which look funny
   > The longest words
   > Pairs of words—general and specific
   > Opposite words
   > Words which sound alike but have different spellings and meanings
   > Words used to greet people
6. Make your own "somebody" book. (See Zolotow's *Someday*.)
7. See what you can do with a crayon. (See Crockett Johnson's *Harold and the Purple Crayon*.)
8. Make your own "very special house." Read Ruth Krauss' *A Very Special House*.
9. Read *Spectacles* by Ellen Raskin. Describe some unusual or imaginary thing you have seen. Also, you might read about imaginary things seen in clouds (Turkle's *The Sky Dog*). Tell about them or write about them. You may want to illustrate the unusual or imaginary things.

LITERATURE—Language

1. Examine books of different genre about night:
   Fantasy
   Folk literature
   Verse story
   Poetry
2. Look for different attitudes toward night found in literature.

3. What is your attitude toward night?
4. Tape or write a night story or poem.
   Make a night book.
   Collect night poems.

LITERATURE—Language

1. Examine different versions of folk tales. Examples:
   Rumpelstiltskin
   > "Rumpelstiltskin" from Arbuthnot's *Time for Old Magic, Tom Tit Tot*, and Zemach's *Duffy and the Devil*.

   Cinderella
   > Clark's *In the Land of Small Dragon;* Grimm's *Cinderella*, illus. Svend Otto S.; Galdone's *Cinderella;* Murphy's *Silver Woven in My Hair;* and Hogrogian's *Cinderella*.

2. Tell how they are alike and how they are different.
3. Make a chart to show the similarities and differences among the different versions.

LITERATURE—Art and Language

1. Explore the art processes of *This Thumbprint* (thumbprinting) and *A Snowy Day* (gum eraser printing).
2. Perhaps you would like to make your own thumbprint book.

LITERATURE—Art

Explore the media used by these illustrators:
> Tissue paper—*Little Blue and Little Yellow*, by Lionni
> Torn paper—*Frederick*, by Lionni
> Pastels—*Always Room For One More*, illustrated by Hogrogian and written by Leodhas
> Scratchboard—*Wynken, Blynken and Nod*, illustrated by Cooney and written by Eugene Field, and *Peter and the Wolf*, illustrated by Frans Haacken and written by Serge Prokofieff
> Multi-media—*Swimmy*, by Lionni
> Photography—*Look Again*, by Hoban

LITERATURE—Language and Art

1. Learn about the author Ezra Jack Keats. Books:
   A Whistle for Willie
   Peter's Chair
   Pet Show!
   A Letter to Amy
   Jennie's Hat
2. Examine the correspondence with Keats. Look at swatches used by Keats in developing his illustrations.
3. Explore the collage process used by Keats in many of his illustrations.

LANGUAGE—Language

1. All of the books listed below are about rides. Some of the rides are make-believe. Others really happened. Which ones are imaginary? Which ones are historical?

    Fritz, Jean. *And Then What Happened, Paul Revere?*
    Haley, Gail E. *Jack Jouette's Ride*
    Lent, Blair. *John Tabor's Ride*
    McCLoskey, Robert. *Burt Dow, Deep-Water Man*

2. Choose a ride in history to tell about. Choose a modern-day ride, and make it into an imaginary tale.

LITERATURE—Language and Art

1. Cardboard printing

    Examine Lent's *The Wave*, written by Hodges, and read the article about his work from *Horn Book* (August, 1965).

2. Linoleum printing

    Examine Brown's *Dick Whittington and His Cat;* Hurd's *Wingfin and Topple*, written by Valens; and Haley's *Jack Jouette's Ride* and *Go Away Stay Away*.

3. Do some printmaking using cardboard, linoleum or other materials. Many different kinds of printmaking are described in Weiss' book *Simple Printmaking.*

LITERATURE—Oral Language and Art

1. Make puppets (Sources of simple puppet-making—Alkema's *Puppet-Making*).
2. Develop a puppet show from a folk tale.

LITERATURE—Oral Language

1. Listen to Ciardi's tape on reading poetry (I Met A Man).
2. Examine newer volumes of poetry.
3. Share some of the newer poetry with the class.

LITERATURE—Language

1. Choose a concept to explore, such as

    Wind—Hatch's *Wind Is To Feel*
    Sand—Cartwright's *Sand*
    Bells—Yolen's *Ring Out!*
    Masks—Baylor's *They Put On Masks*

2. Find different types of literature (i.e., factual, fiction, folklore, poetry) dealing with a concept. Extend the experience with the concept to as many areas of the curriculum as possible (i.e., science, mathematics, social studies, fine arts, language arts, physical education).

LITERATURE—Media and Language

1. Listen to tape of an interview with author Marguerite Henry.
2. Read *Dear Readers and Riders*.

   Books accompanying tape.

   > *Born To Trot*
   > *Misty of Chincoteague*
   > *Stormy, Misty's Foal*
   > *White Stallion of Lipizza*
   > *King of the Wind*
   > *Brighty of Grand Canyon*
   > *Album of Horses*
   > *Mustang, Wild Spirit of the West*
   > *Justin Morgan Had a Horse*
   > *Benjamin West and His Cat Grimalkin*
   > *Cinabar, the One O'Clock Fox*
   > *Mustang*

3. Listen to tapes *From the Mixed-Up Files of Mrs. Basil E. Frankweiler*, by Konigsburg, or *The Cricket in Times Square*, by Selden. You might like to compare and contrast the taped version of a story with the book.

LITERATURE—Language

1. Examine some of the books from the new book collection.
2. Share a new book with the class. (You might want to examine the envelope which contains ideas for sharing books.)

LITERATURE—Language

1. Read *Red Riding Hood*, by deRegniers.
2. Dramatize. (You might want to use the costume box.)

LITERATURE—Language

1. Read concrete poetry from *Seeing Things*, by Robert Froman; *Concrete Is Not Always Hard*, by A. Barbara Pilon; and *Poems Make Pictures Pictures Make Poems*, by Rimanelli and Pimsleur.
2. Make a concrete poem.

LITERATURE—Oral Language

   Examine Lynd Ward's *The Silver Pony*. Then tell the story while looking at the illustrations.

LITERATURE—Language

1. Compare the themes of Peet's *The Spooky Tale of Prewitt Peacock* and Wildsmith's *The Little Wood Duck*.
2. Compare the themes of Massie's *Dazzle* and Duvoisin's *Petunia*.
3. Then contrast the themes of both groups of books.

LITERATURE—Language and Art

1. Ask seven people or seven small groups of people to participate in this activity. Give each person or group one of the parts of the book *An Aminal*, by Balian.
2. Read your part of the book. Talk about it and then illustrate it.
3. Then read the eighth part of the story.

LITERATURE—Language Art

1. These books tell about different kinds of hats:
   The Marcel Marceau Counting Book by George Mendoza
   My Closet Full of Hats by Harvey Weiss
   Choose a hat box and develop a story about the person who would wear that hat. You might want to dramatize the story. Each member of a small group might choose a hat box and make up a story using the characters suggested by the hats. The story could be taped or dramatized.
2. These stories are about fancy hats:
   Jennie's Hat by Ezra Jack Keats
   Jasmine by Roger Duvoisin
3. Where are tall black hats worn?
   How are they used?
   You might like to tell or write a story about a tall black hat.
   These stories are about tall black hats:
   Sumi's Prize by Yoshiko Uchida
   The Hat by Tomi Ungerer
4. Choose a hat from the box. Tape or write a story about an adventure with the hat. These stories are about adventures with hats:
   Herman's Hats by George Mendoza
   The 500 Hats of Bartholomew Cubbins by Dr. Seuss
   Sumi's Prize by Yoshiko Uchida

LITERATURE—Language, Music, and Art

1. Read Horwitz's *When the Sky Is Like Lace*.
2. Choose an activity.

Language

What do you think would be good to eat on a bimulous night?
Make up some rules you should follow on a bimulous night.
What presents would you give on a bimulous night?
What activities might you like to do on a bimulous night?

Music

   Compose a tune for the new song "The Katydid."
   Write a song for the snails to use in reply to the otters.
   Write a song which is not nasty for the otters to sing to the snails.

Art

   Draw a bimulous night.

LITERATURE—Art, Language, Music, and Movement

1. Read Byrd Baylor's *They Put on Masks*.

   "Now
   think
   what kind of mask
   your mask
   would be.

   And think
   what kind of songs
   that mask would bring
   out of you . . .

   and what strange
   unknown dances
   your bones
   would
   remember

   and what you would ask
   and what you would promise

   Now think
   what kind of mask
   your mask
   would be."

2. Make a mask. Perhaps you could find music which would accompany your movement while wearing the mask.
3. Alkema's *Masks* gives information on mask making.
4. More information about masks can be found in *Masks and Mask Makers*, by Kari Hunt and Bernice Wells Carlson, and *The Mystery of Masks*, by Christine Price.
5. In Chapter 2 of Yep's *Child of the Owl*, there is an interesting account of an owl mask.

LITERATURE—Art and Creative Dramatics

1. Read *Who's in Rabbit's House?* written by Verna Aardema and illustrated by Leo and Diane Dillon.
2. Make masks and act out the story. Alkema's *Masks* contains information about mask making.

LITERATURE—Language and Art

1. Examine the book *Thirteen,* by Remy Charlip and Jerry Joyner.
2. Choose a number, perhaps less than thirteen, and make a book.

LITERATURE—Music

1. Read Wilson Gage's *Down in the Boondocks.*
2. Compose music to accompany the verse.

LITERATURE—Construction Activities and Language

1. Examine Macaulay's books (*Pyramid, Cathedral, Castle,* and others).
2. Take boxes and/or blocks and construct a building.

LITERATURE—Art

1. Read Rumer Godden's *The Kitchen Madonna.*
2. From scraps, make an icon.

LITERATURE—Creative Language

1. Read Kroll's *The Tyrannosaurus Game.*
2. Begin your own "add-on" story. Start the story on a tape or on a piece of chart paper or wrapping paper. Ask your classmates to help develop the story.
3. Another book which has games to play with your classmates is Anne Rockwell's *Games.*

LITERATURE—Oral Language

1. Read some riddle books. (Interesting riddle books are *What a Riddle Book, The Monster Riddle Book*, and *Giants,* written by Jane Sarnoff and Reynold Ruffins)
2. Prepare to share a few riddles with the class.

LITERATURE—Listening

1. Listen to the tape of Karla Kuskin's *A Boy Had A Mother Who Bought Him A Hat.*
2. As the tape plays again, put pieces on the flannelboard as the boy receives his gifts.

LITERATURE—Oral Language

1. Read sone of Lobel's Frog and Toad books.
2. Tape a dialogue between frog and toad.
3. You might like to make up a new conversation between frog and toad.

LITERATURE—Creative Language

1. Read Kohn's *How High Is Up?*
2. Make up your own questions and answers.
3. You might want to make a packet of questions for your classmates to answer. The packet could be part of the independent learning center.

LITERATURE—Creative Language

1. Read Burningham's *Come Away From the Water, Shirley.*
2. Make up a story which has two parts happening at the same time (a parallel plot).

LITERATURE—Language

1. Read Byrd Baylor's *Guess Who My Favorite Person Is.*
2. With one or more of your classmates, play the Tell-What-Your Favorite-Thing-Is Game. You might want to tape parts of your game or make a book about your game.

LITERATURE—Art and Creative Language

1. Select a poem from Jack Prelutsky's *The Snopp on the Sidewalk,* and illustrate it.
2. Make up your own imaginary person or thing. Tape or write your story. You may want to make a model or an illustration of it.

LITERATURE—Language and Art

1. Read *The Bunyip of Berkeley's Creek,* written by Jenny Wagner and illustrated by Ron Brooks, and "The Oopik" in *Alligator Pie,* by Dennis.
2. Create a story or poem about an imaginary creature. You might want to illustrate it or develop a model of it.

LITERATURE—Language and Music

1. Read Langstaff's *Hot Cross Buns and Other Street Cries.*
2. What message would you like to send in a song? What idea would you like to advertise through song?
3. Make up a singing message or an advertisement.

LITERATURE—Language, Music, Art, and Dance

1. Read *The Way To Start a Day,* by Byrd Baylor.
2. Develop a special way to start a day.

LITERATURE—Language

1. Read *The Other Way To Listen,* by Byrd Baylor. Choose something special to observe and listen to. You might want to select a picture to help you think about an idea or an emotion.
2. Read *The Paint-Box Sea* by Doris Lund. The children in the story learn a great deal about the sea. After you have observed and/or thought about an idea, you might like to write a haiku poem or a cinquain poem:

Haiku poetry

Line 1	5 syllables
Line 2	7 syllables
Line 3	5 syllables

Cinquain poetry

Line 1	one word
Line 2	two words about the word on the first line
Line 3	three words about the word on the first line
Line 4	four words about the word on the first line
Line 5	a synonym or a summary word related to the word on Line 1

LITERATURE—Language and Art

1. Read Anno's *The King's Flower*. Imagine ordinary objects in the classroom to be very large in size. You might like to illustrate your ideas.
2. Read poems from Worth's *Still More Small Poems*. Find a picture of an ordinary thing and compose a small poem about it.

LITERATURE—Language and Art

1. Read Allard's *Bumps in the Night*.
2. Tape the story, putting in sound effects.

LITERATURE—Language

1. Read Tresselt's *What Did You Leave Behind?*
2. Choose an interesting experience you have had. Tell or write about what you left behind, including what you saw, heard, smelled, tasted, and touched.

LITERATURE—Language

1. Read Sharmat's *I Am Not A Pest*.
2. Tell or write about how to be a genuine pest.

LITERATURE—Art

1. Read McDermott's *Anansi the Spider* and Moore's poem "Spider" in *Little Raccoon and Poems From the Woods*.
2. Take the yarn and string box and make a web in the room or on the playground.

LITERATURE—Language

1. Read Mercer Mayer's *Mrs. Beggs and the Wizard* to the marked part.
2. Then supply your own ending. Who or what do you think was at the door? Why was the person or thing at the door?

LITERATURE—Language

1. Look at *Magical Changes* by Graham Oakley.
2. Choose a combination of illustrations and tell or write about it.

LITERATURE—Art and Language

1. Read *Bear Hunt* by Anthony Browne.
2. Choose a problem to draw your way out of. Tell or write about your experience.

LITERATURE—Language

1. Read *The Good Thing the Bad Thing* by Thomas.
2. Choose a familiar situation and consider the good side of it and the bad side of it. Tape or write your response.

LITERATURE—Language

1. Read *One Big Wish* by Williams.
2. Make one big wish and tell or write what happened.

LITERATURE—Language and Art
1. Read Barrett's *Animals Should Definitely "Not" Act Like People.*
2. Choose an animal and tell how it should not act like people. See if you can use alliteration in your story. You may wish to illustrate your story.

LITERATURE—Art and Language
1. Read Bornstein's *I'll Draw a Meadow.*
2. Choose a setting and draw yourself in it. You may want to tell or write about the experience you have created.

Bibliography

Aardema, Verna. *Who's in the Rabbit's House?,* illus. Leo and Diane Dillon. New York: Dial Press, 1975.

Adoff, Arnold. *Ma nDa La,* illus. Emily McCully. New York: Harper and Row, 1971.

Alkema, Chester Jay. *Masks.* New York: Sterling Publishing Company, 1971.

————. *Puppet-Making.* New York: Sterling Publishing Company, 1971.

Allard, Barry. *Bumps in the Night.* Garden City, N.Y.: Doubleday and Company, 1979.

Anno, Mitsumasa. *The King's Flower.* New York: Collins, 1978.

Arbuthnot, May Hill, and Mark Taylor. *Time for Old Magic.* Chicago: Scott Foresman and Company, 1969.

Atwood, Ann. *Haiku-Vision.* New York: Charles Scribner's Sons, 1977.

Balian, Lorna. *An Aminal.* Nashville: Abingdon Press, 1972.

Barrett, Judi. *Animals Should Definitely "Not" Act Like People,* illus. Ron Barrett. New York: Atheneum, 1980.

Baylor, Byrd. *Guess Who My Favorite Person Is,* illus. Robert Andrew Parks. New York: Charles Scribner's Sons, 1977.

————. *They Put on Masks,* illus. Jerry Ingram. New York: Charles Scribner's Sons, 1974.

————. *The Way To Start a Day,* illus. Peter Parnell. New York: Charles Scribner's Sons, 1978.

Baylor, Byrd, and Peter Parnall. *The Other Way To Listen.* New York: Charles Scribner's Sons, 1978.

Behn, Harry, trans. *Cricket Songs.* New York: Harcourt Brace Jovanovich, 1964.

Bornstein, Ruth Lercher. *I'll Draw a Meadow.* New York: Harper and Row, 1979.

Brown, Marcia. *Dick Whittington and His Cat.* New York: Charles Scribner's Sons, 1950.

Browne, Anthony. *Bear Hunt.* New York: Atheneum, 1980.

Burningham, John. *Come Away From the Water, Shirley.* New York: Thomas Y. Crowell Company, 1977.

————. *Mr. Gumpy's Outing.* New York: Holt, Rinehart and Winston, 1971.

————. *Would You Rather . . .* New York: Thomas Y. Crowell Company, 1978.

Cartwright, Sally. *Sand,* photo. Don Madden. New York: Coward, McCann and Geoghegan, 1975.

Charlip, Remy. *Fortunately.* New York: Parents' Magazine Press, 1964.

Charlip, Remy, and Jerry Joyner. *Thirteen.* New York: Parents' Magazine Press, 1975.

Ciardi, John. *I Met a Man.* Boston: Houghton Mifflin Company, 1961.

Clark, Ann Nolan. *In the Land of Small Dragon,* illus. Tony Chen. New York: Viking Press, 1979.

Daughtery, James. *Andy and the Lion.* New York: Viking Press, 1938.

de Regniers, Beatrice Schenk. *Red Riding Hood,* illus. Edward Gorey. New York: Atheneum, 1972.

Drawson, Blair. *I Like Hats!* Aginocourt: Ontario: Scholastic—TAB Publications, 1977.

Duff, Maggie. *Rum Pum Pum.* New York: Macmillan Publishing Company, 1978.

Duvoisin, Roger. *Jasmine.* New York: Alfred A. Knopf, 1973.

————. *Petunia.* New York: Alfred A. Knopf, 1950.

Fatio, Louise. *The Happy Lion,* illus. Roger Duvoisin. New York: McGraw-Hill Book Company, 1954.

Field, Eugene. *Wynken, Blynken, and Nod,* illus. Barbara Cooney. New York: Hastings House, 1964.

Freeman, Don. *Dandelion.* New York: Viking Press, 1964.

Fritz, Jean. *And Then What Happened, Paul Revere?* illus. Margot Tomes. New York: Coward, McCann and Geoghegan, 1973.

Froman, Robert. *Seeing Things.* New York: Thomas Y. Crowell Company, 1974.

Haley, Gail E. *Jack Jouette's Ride.* New York: Viking Press, 1973.

Hatch, Shirley Cook. *Wind Is To Feel.* New York: Coward, McCann and Geoghegan, 1973.

Henry, Marguerite. *Album of Horses.* Chicago: Rand McNally and Company, 1951.

————. *Benjamin West and His Cat Grimalkin.* Indianapolis: Bobbs-Merrill Company, 1947.

————. *Born To Trot.* Chicago: Rand McNally and Company, 1950.

————. *Brighty of Grand Canyon.* Chicago: Rand McNally and Company, 1954.

————. *Cinnabar, the One O'Clock Fox.* Chicago, Rand McNally and Company, 1956.

————. *Dear Readers and Riders.* Chicago: Rand McNally and Company, 1969.

————. *Justin Morgan Had a Horse.* Chicago: Rand McNally and Company, 1954.

————. *King of the Wind.* Chicago: Rand McNally and Company, 1948.

————. *Misty of Chincoteague.* Chicago: Rand McNally and Company, 1947.

————. *Mustang, Wild Spirit of the West.* Chicago: Rand McNally and Company, 1966.

————. *Stormy, Misty's Foal.* Chicago: Rand McNally and Company, 1963.

————. *White Stallion of Lipizza.* Chicago: Rand McNally and Company, 1964.

Hoban, Tana. *Look Again.* New York: Macmillan Publishing Company, 1971.

Hodges, Margaret. *The Wave,* illus. Blair Lent. Boston: Houghton Mifflin Company, 1964.

Hogrogian, Nonny. *Cinderella.* New York: Greenwillow Books, 1981.

Horwitz, Elinor. *When the Sky Is Like Lace,* illus. Barbara Cooney. Philadelphia: J.B. Lippincott Company, 1975.

Hunt, Kari, and Bernice Wells Carlson. *Masks and Mask Makers.* Nashville: Abingdon Press, 1961.

Hutchins, Pat. *Rosie's Walk.* New York: Macmillan Publishing Company, 1968.

Johnson, Crockett. *Harold and the Purple Crayon.* New York: Harper and Row, 1958.

Keats, Ezra Jack. *Jennie's Hat*. New York: Harper and Row, 1966.

———. *A Letter to Amy*. New York: Harper and Row, 1968.

———. *Pet Show!* New York: Macmillan Publishing Company, 1972.

———. *Peter's Chair*. New York: Harper and Row, 1967.

———. *The Snowy Day*. New York: Viking Press, 1962.

———. *A Whistle for Willie*. New York: Viking Press, 1964.

Kohn, Bernice. *How High Is Up?* illus. Jan Pyk. New York: G.P. Putnam's Sons, 1971.

Konigsburg, E. L. *From the Mixed-Up Files of Mrs. Basil E. Frankweiler*. New York: Atheneum, 1969.

Krauss, Ruth. *This Thumbprint*. New York: Harper and Row, 1967.

———. *A Very Special House,* illus. Maurice Sendak. New York: Harper and Row, 1953.

Kroll, Steven. *The Tyrannosaurus Game,* illus. Tomie de Paola. New York: Holiday House, 1976.

Kuskin, Karla. *A Boy Had a Mother Who Bought Him a Hat*. Boston: Houghton Mifflin Company, 1976.

Lee, Dennis. *Alligator Pie*. Boston: Houghton Mifflin Company, 1975.

Lionni, Leo. *Little Blue and Little Yellow*. New York: Ivan Odolensky, 1959.

———. *Frederick*. N.Y. Pantheon Books, 1967.

———. *Swimmy*. New York: Pantheon Books, 1973.

Little Red Riding Hood, illus. Warja Honegger-Lavater. New York: Museum of Modern Art, 1965.

Lobel, Arnold. *Frog and Toad Are Friends*. New York: Harper and Row, 1970.

———. *Frog and Toad Together*. New York: Harper and Row, 1972.

Longstaff, John. *Hot Cross Buns and Other Old Street Cries*. New York: Atheneum, 1977.

Lund, Doris Herald. *The Paint-Box Sea,* illus. Symeon Shimin. New York: McGraw-Hill Book Company, 1973.

Macauley, David. *Castle*. Boston: Houghton Mifflin Company, 1977.

———. *Cathedral*. Boston: Houghton Mifflin Company, 1973.

———. *Pyramid*. Boston: Houghton Mifflin Company, 1975.

Massie, Diane Redfield. *Dazzle*. New York: Parents' Magazine Press, 1969.

Mayer, Mercer. *Mrs. Beggs and the Wizard*. New York: Parents' Magazine Press, 1973.

McCloskey, Robert. *Burt Dow, Deep-Water Man*. New York: Viking Press, 1963.

McDermott, Gerald. *Anansi the Spider*. New York: Holt, Rinehart and Winston, 1972.

Mendoza, George. *Herman's Hats,* illus. Frank Bozzo. Garden City, N.Y.: Doubleday and Company, 1969.

———. *The Marcel Marceau Counting Book,* photo. Milton H. Greene. Garden City, N.Y.: Doubleday and Company, 1971.

Mizumura, Kazue. *Flower Moon Snow*. New York: Thomas Y. Crowell Company, 1977.

Moore, Lillian. *Little Raccoon and Poems From the Woods*. New York: McGraw-Hill Book Company, 1975.

Murphy, Shirley Rousseau. *Silver Woven in My Hair*. New York: Atheneum, 1977.

Ness, Evaline. *Tom Tit Tot*. New York: Charles Scribner's Sons, 1965.

O'Neill, Mary. *Hailstones and Halibut Bones,* illus. Leonard Weisgard. Garden City, N.Y.: Doubleday and Company, 1961.

Peet, Bill. *The Spooky Tail of Prewitt Peacock.* Boston: Houghton Mifflin Company, 1972.

Pilon, A. Barbara. *Concrete Is Not Always Hard.* Columbus, O.: Xerox Education Publications, 1972.

Prelutsky, Jack. *The Snopp on the Sidewalk,* illus. Byron Barton. New York: William Morrow and Company, 1977.

Price, Christine. *The Mystery of Masks.* New York: Charles Scribner's Sons, 1978.

Prokofieff, Serge. *Peter and the Wolf,* illus. Frans Haachen. New York: Franklin Watts, 1961.

Raskin, Ellen. *Spectacles.* New York: Atheneum, 1968.

Rimanelli, Griose, and Paul Pimsleur. *Poems Make Pictures and Pictures Make Poems.* New York: Pantheon Books, 1972.

Rockwell, Ann. *Games.* New York: Thomas Y. Crowell, 1973.

Sarnoff, Jane, and Reynold Ruffins. *Giants!* New York: Charles Scribner's Sons, 1977.

————. *The Monster Riddle Book.* New York: Charles Scribner's Sons, 1978.

————. *What a Riddle Book!* New York: Charles Scribner's Sons, 1974.

Seldon, George. *The Cricket in Times Square.* New York: Farrar, Straus and Giroux, 1960.

Seuss, Dr. *The 500 Hats of Bartholomew Cubbins.* New York: Vanguard Press, 1938.

Sharmat, Marjorie, and Mitchell Sharmat. *I Am Not a Pest,* illus. Diane Dawson. New York: E.P. Dutton and Company, 1979.

Thomas, Karen. *The Good Thing the Bad Thing,* illus. Yaroslava. Englewood Cliffs, N.J.: Prentice-Hall, 1979.

Tresselt, Alvin. *What Did You Leave Behind?* illus. Roger Duvoisin. New York: Lothrop, Lee and Shephard, 1978.

Turkel, Brinton. *The Sky Dog.* New York: Viking Press, 1969.

Uchida, Yoshiko. *Sumi's Prize,* illus. Kazue Mizumura. New York: Charles Scribner's Sons, 1964.

Ungerer, Tomi. *The Hat.* New York: Parents' Magazine Press, 1970.

Valens, Evans G. *Wingfin and Topple,* illus. Clement Hurd. Cleveland: World Publishing Company, 1962.

Wagner, Jenny. *The Bunyip of Berkeley's Creek,* illus. Ron Brooks. Scarsdale, N.Y.: Bradbury Press, 1973.

Ward, Lynd. *The Silver Pony.* Boston: Houghton Mifflin Company, 1973.

Weiss, Harvey. *My Closet Full of Hats.* New York: Abelard-Schuman, 1962.

Weiss, Peter. *Simple Printmaking,* illus. Sally Grulla. New York: Lothrop, Lee and Shephard, 1976.

Wildsmith, Brian. *The Little Wood Duck.* New York: Franklin Watts, 1973.

Williams, Jay. *One Big Wish,* illus. John O'Brien. New York: Macmillan Publishing Company, 1980.

Worth, Valerie. *Still More Small Peoms,* illus. Natalie Babbit. New York: Farrar, Straus and Giroux, 1978.

Yep, Laurence. *Child of the Owl.* New York: Harper and Row, 1977.

Yolen, Jane. *Ring Out!* New York: Seabury Press, 1974.

Zemach, Harve and Margot. *Duffy and the Devil.* New York: Farrar, Straus and Giroux, 1973.

Zolotow, Charlotte. *Someday,* illus. Arnold Lobel. New York: Harper and Row, 1964.

Appendix J
Picture Books with No Text or Minimal Text

Picture Books Without Words

Alexander, Martha. *Blackboard Bear*. New York: Dial Press, 1977.

———. *Bobo's Dream*. New York: Dial Press, 1970.

———. *Out! Out! Out!* New York: Dial Press, 1968.

Anno, Mitsumasa. *Anno's Italy*. New York: Collins, 1979.

———. *Anno's Journey*. New York: Collier-World, 1977.

Ardizzone, Edward. *The Wrong Side of the Bed*. Garden City, N.Y.: Doubleday and Company, 1970.

Bang, Molly. *The Grey Lady and the Strawberry Snatcher*. New York: Four Winds Press, 1980.

Baum, Willi. *Birds of a Feather*. Reading, Mass.: Addison-Wesley, 1969.

Carle, Eric. *1, 2, 3 to the Zoo*. New York: World Publishing Company, 1968.

Carroll, Ruth. *The Christmas Kitten*. New York: Henry Z. Walck, 1970.

———. *The Witch Kitten*. New York: Henry Z. Walck, 1970.

Charlip, Remy, and Jerry Joyner. *Thirteen*. New York: Parents' Magazine Press, 1975.

DeGroat, Diane. *Alligator's Toothache*. New York: Crown Publishers, 1977.

de Paola, Tomie. *Flicks*. New York: Harcourt Brace Jovanovich, 1979.

———. *Pancakes for Breakfast*. New York: Harcourt Brace Jovanovich, 1978.

Giovannetti. *Max*. New York: Atheneum, 1977.

Goodall, John S. *Adventures of Paddy Pork*. New York: Harcourt, Brace and World, 1968.

———. *The Ballooning Adventures of Paddy Pork*. New York: Harcourt, Brace and World, 1969.

———. *Jacko*. New York: Harcourt, Brace and World, 1971.

———. *The Midnight Adventures of Kelly, Dot, and Esmeralda*. New York: Atheneum, 1972.

———. *Paddy's New Hat*. New York: Atheneum, 1980.

———. *The Surprise Picnic*. New York: Atheneum, 1977.

Hamberger, John. *A Sleepless Day*. New York: Four Winds Press, 1973.

Hauptman, Tatjana. *A Day in the Life of Petronella Pig*. New York: Sunflower Books, 1978.

———. *The Lazy Dog*. New York: Four Winds Press, 1971.

Heller, Linda. *Lily at the Table*. New York: Macmillan Publishing Company, 1979.

Hoban, Tana. *Look Again*. New York: Macmillan Publishing Company, 1971.

Hogrogian, Nonny. *Apples*. New York: Macmillan Publishing Company, 1971.

Hutchins, Pat. *Changes, Changes*. New York: Macmillan Publishing Company, 1971.

Keats, Ezra Jack. *Psst! Doggie*. New York: Franklin Watts, 1973.

Kent, Jack. *The Egg Book*. New York: Macmillan Publishing Company, 1975.

Krahn, Fernando. *Catch That Cat!* New York: E.P. Dutton and Company, 1978.

————. *Here Comes Alex Pumpernickel.* Boston: Little, Brown and Company, 1981.

————. *Little Love Story.* Philadelphia: J.B. Lippincott Company, 1976.

————. *The Mystery of the Giant Footprints.* New York: E.P. Dutton and Company, 1977.

————. *Who's Seen the Scissors?* New York: E.P. Dutton and Company, 1975.

Macmillan, Bruce. *The Alphabet Symphony.* New York: William Morrow and Company, 1977.

Mari, Iela. *The Magic Balloon.* New York: S.G. Phillips, 1967.

————. *Eat and Be Eaten.* Woodbury, N.Y.: Baron's Educational Series, 1980.

Mayer, Mercer. *A Boy, a Dog, and a Frog.* New York: Dial Press, 1967.

————. *Frog Goes to Dinner.* New York: Dial Press, 1974.

————. *Frog on His Own.* New York: Dial Press, 1973.

————. *Frog, Where Are You?* New York: Dial Press, 1969.

————. *The Great Cat Chase.* New York: Four Winds Press, 1974.

————. *Hiccup.* New York: Dial Press, 1976.

————. *One Frog Too Many.* New York: Dial Press, 1975.

————. *Two Moral Tales.* New York: Four Winds Press, 1974.

Mordillo, Guillermo. *The Damp and Daffy Doings of a Daring Pirate Ship.* New York: Harlin Quist, 1971.

Oakley, Graham. *Magical Changes.* New York: Atheneum, 1979.

Ringi, Kjell. *The Magic Stick.* New York: Harper and Row, 1968.

————. *The Winner.* New York: Harper and Row, 1969.

Simmons, Ellie. *Wheels.* New York: David McKay Company, 1969.

Spier, Peter. *Noah's Ark.* Garden City, N.Y.: Doubleday and Company, 1977.

Thaler, Mike. *There's a Hippopotamus Under My Bed,* illus. Ray Cruz. New York: Franklin Watts, 1977.

Turkle, Brinton. *Deep in the Forest.* New York: E.P. Dutton and Company, 1976.

Ueno, Noriko. *Elephant Buttons.* New York: Harper and Row, 1973.

Ungarer, Tomi. *Snail, Where Are You?* New York: Harper and Row, 1962.

Ward, Lynd. *The Silver Pony.* Boston: Houghton Mifflin Company, 1973.

Wezel, Peter. *The Good Bird.* New York: Harper and Row, 1966.

Wildsmith, Brian. *Circus.* New York: Franklin Watts, 1970.

Winter, Paul. *Sir Andrew.* New York: Crown Publishers, 1980.

Picture Books With Minimal Text

Anno, Mitsumasa. *Upside-Downers.* New York: Weatherhill, 1971.

Aruego, Jose. *Look What I Can Do.* New York: Charles Scribner's Sons, 1971.

Baker, Alan. *Benjamin and the Box.* Philadelphia: J.B. Lippincott Company, 1977.

Balian, Lorna. *Bah! Hambug?* Nashville: Abingdon, 1977.

Banchek, Lina. *Snake In, Snake Out,* illus. Elaine Arnold. New York: Thomas Y. Crowell Company, 1978.

Barton, Byron. *Buzz Buzz Buzz.* New York: Macmillan Publishing Company, 1973.

Boynston, Sandra. *If at First . . .* Boston: Little, Brown and Company, 1980.

Browne, Anthony. *Bear Hunt*. New York: Atheneum, 1980.

Burningham, John. *Mr. Gumpy's Outing*. New York: Holt, Rinehart and Winston, 1971.

Cameron, John. *If Mice Could Fly*. New York: Atheneum, 1979.

de Paola, Tomie. *The Knight and the Dragon*. New York: G.P. Putnam's Sons, 1980.

Ginsburg, Mirra. *Good Morning, Chick,* illus. Bryon Barton. New York: Greenwillow Books, 1980.

———. *The Strongest One of All,* Jose Aruego and Ariane Dewey. New York: William Morrow and Company, 1977.

Himler, Robert. *Wake Up, Jeremiah*. New York: Harper and Row, 1979.

Hoban, Tana. *Where Is It?* New York: Macmillan Publishing Company, 1974.

Hoffman, Hilde. *The Green Grass Grows All Around*. New York: Macmillan Publishing Company, 1968.

Hutchins, Pat. *Rosie's Walk*. New York: Macmillan Publishing Company, 1968.

Kalan, Robert. *Blue Sea,* illus. Donald Crews. New York: Greenwillow Books, 1979.

Krahn, Fernando. *Gustavus and Stop*. New York: E.P. Dutton and Company, 1969.

Kraus, Robert. *Whose Mouse Are You?* Macmillan Publishing Company, 1970.

———. *The Lion and the Mouse,* illus. Ed Young. Garden City, N.Y.: Doubleday and Company, 1979.

Lobel, Arnold. *On Market Street,* illus. Anita Lobel. New York: Greenwillow Books, 1981.

Maestro, Betsy, and Ginlio Maestro. *Busy Day*. New York: Crown Publishers, 1978.

Parnall, Peter. *The Mountain*. Garden City, N.Y.: Doubleday and Company, 1971.

Paterson, Diane. *The Biggest Snowstorm Ever*. New York: Dial Press, 1974.

Richter, Mischa. *Quack?* New York: Harper and Row, 1978.

Schermer, Judith. *Mouse in House*. Boston: Houghton Mifflin Company, 1979.

Shector, Ben. *Conrad's Castle*. New York: Harper and Row, 1967.

Smith, Mr. and Mrs. *The Long Slide*. New York: Atheneum, 1977.

Tensen, Ruth M. *Come to the Zoo*. New York: Reilly and Lee, 1948.

Waber, Bernard. *The Snake*. Boston: Houghton Mifflin Company, 1978.

Wildsmith, Brian. *Puzzles*. New York: Franklin Watts, 1970.

Zolotow, Charlotte. *Some Things Go Together*. New York: Abelard-Schuman, 1969.

Appendix K
Sources of High Interest, Easy Reading

YR
011
E
Elementary School Library Collection. Published annually by Bro-Dart.
      Gives interest level and reading level.

YR
028
Rosenburg and Rosenburg. *Young People's Literature in Series.* Vol. I and II.
      Published by Libraries Unlimited, Littleton, Colorado.
      Annotated.

YR
028
S
Sutherland. *The Best in Children's Books.* Published by University of Chicago
      Press.
      Contains index to reading levels.

YR
028
W
Book Bait. Published by American Library Association.

YR
028
5
Reading Aids Series. Published by Garrard Publishing Company.
      Spache. *Good Reading for Poor Readers.*
      Graves. *Easy Reading: Book Series and Periodicals for Less Able Read-
        ers.* 1979.

YR
016
R
Reid. *Reading Ladders for Human Relations.* Published by American Council
      on Education.

YR
028
L
Larrick. *Teacher's Guide to Children's Books.* Published by Charles E. Merrill
      Books.

YR
028
N
High Interest, Easy Reading. Published by National Council of Teachers of
      English. Third edition, 1979. For junior and senior high school students.

Section on high interest, easy reading in these periodicals:
    School Library Journal.
    Book List

Periodical.
    The High/Low Report. Started in 1979. 10 issues per year.
      20 Waterside Plaza, N.Y., N.Y. 10010, $10.50 per year.

Appendix L
Books to Read Aloud to Older Children

Alexander, Lloyd. *The First Two Lives of Lukas-Kaska*. New York: E. P. Dutton and Company, 1978.

Allan, Mabel Esther. *Bridge of Friendship*. New York: Dodd, Mead and Company, 1955.

Alter, Judy. *After Pa Was Shot*. New York: William Morrow and Company, 1978.

Anderson, Margaret J. *Searching for Shina*. New York: Alfred A. Knopf, 1977.

Arthur, Ruth M. *An Old Magic*. New York: Atheneum, 1977.

Avi. *The History of Helpless Harry*. New York: Pantheon Books, 1980.

———. *Upham's Revenge*. New York: Holt, Rinehart and Winston, 1976.

Babbitt, Natalie. *The Eyes of the Amaryllis*. New York: Farrar, Straus and Giroux, 1977.

Bawden, Nina. *Rebel in a Rock*. Philadelphia: J. B. Lippincott Company, 1978.

Beatty, John, and Patricia Beatty. *Master Rosalind*. New York: William Morrow and Company, 1974.

———. *Hail Columbia*. New York: William Morrow and Company, 1970.

———. *Something To Shout About*. New York: William Morrow and Company, 1976.

Bell, Frederic. *Jenny's Corner*. New York: Random House, 1974.

Beresford, Elisabeth. *Invisible Magic*. London: Hart-Davis, 1974.

Berstein, Margery, and Janet Kobrin. *The Summer Maker*. New York: Charles Scribner's Sons, 1977.

Bickham, Jack M. *Dinah, Blow Your Horn*. Garden City, N.Y.: Doubleday and Company, 1976.

Blume, Judy. *Freckle Juice*. New York: Four Winds Press, 1971.

Bodker, Cecil. *Silas and the Black Mare*. New York: Delacorte Press, 1978.

Brink, Carol Ryrie. *The Bad Times of Irma Baumlein*. New York: Macmillan Publishing Company, 1972.

Buchwald, Emilie. *Gildaen*. New York: Harcourt, Brace and Jovanovich, 1973.

Burch, Robert. *Wilkin's Ghost*. New York: Viking Press, 1978.

Burchard, Peter. *Digger*. New York: G. P. Putnam's Sons, 1980.

Burn, Doris. *The Tale of Lazy Lizard*. New York: G. P. Putnam's Sons, 1977.

Byars, Betsy. *The 18th Emergency*. New York: Viking Press, 1973.

Callan, Larry. *The Deadly Mandrake*. Boston: Little, Brown and Company, 1978.

Calvert, Patricia. *Snowbird*. New York: Charles Scribner's Sons, 1980.

Cameron, Eleanor. *The Court of the Stone Children*. New York: E. P. Dutton and Company, 1973.

———. *Julia and the Hand of God*. New York: E. P. Dutton and Company, 1977.

Christopher, John. *Wild Jack*. New York: Macmillan Publishing Company, 1974.

Clifford, Eth. *The Curse of the Moonraker*. Boston: Houghton Mifflin Company, 1977.

Cooper, Susan. *The Dark Is Rising*. New York: Atheneum, 1973.

Corcoran, Barbara. *The Long Journey*. New York: Atheneum, 1970.

Coren, Alan. *Arthur the Kid*. Boston: Little, Brown and Company, 1977.

Crayden, Dorothy. *The Riddles of Mermaid House*. New York: Atheneum, 1977.

Crowley, Jay. *The Silent One*. New York: Alfred A. Knopf, 1981.

de Roo, Anne. *Cinnamon and Nutmeg*. Nashville: Thomas Nelson, 1972.

Fechner, Constance. *The Link Boys*. New York: Farrar, Straus and Giroux, 1971.

Fife, Dale. *North of Danger*. New York: E. P. Dutton and Company, 1978.

Fisher, Leonard Everett. *Sweeny's Ghost*. Garden City, N.Y.: Doubleday and Company, 1975.

Fitzgerald, John D. *The Great Brain Does It Again,* illus. Mercer Mayer. New York: Dial Press, 1975.

———. *The Great Brain Reforms*. New York: Dial Press, 1973.

Fleischman, Sid. *Humbug Mountain*. Boston: Little, Brown and Company, 1978.

Flory, Jane. *It Was a Pretty Good Year*. Boston: Houghton Mifflin Company, 1977.

Gessner, Lynne. *To See a Witch*. Nashville: Thomas Nelson, 1978.

Giff, Patricia Reilly. *Have You Seen Hyacinth Macaw?* New York: Delacorte Press, 1981.

Gipson, Fred. *Little Arliss*. New York: Harper and Row, 1978.

Greene, Constance C. *Isabelle the Itch*. New York: Viking Press, 1973.

Greenwald, Sheila. *The Mariah Delaney Lending Library Disaster*. Boston: Houghton Mifflin Company, 1977.

Griffiths, Helen. *Running Wild*. New York: Holiday House, 1977.

Hoover, H. M. *The Lost Star*. New York: Viking Press, 1979.

Hunter, Mollie. *The Haunted Mountain*. New York: Harper and Row, 1972.

———. *The Walking Stone*. New York: Harper and Row, 1972.

Karl, Jean. *Beloved Benjamin Is Waiting*. New York: E. P. Dutton and Company, 1972.

Keith, Harold. *The Obstinate Land*. New York: Thomas Y. Crowell Company, 1977.

Lampman, Evelyn Sibley. *Bargain Bride*. New York: Atheneum, 1977.

Lasker, Joe. *The Strange Voyage of Neptune's Car*. New York: Viking Press, 1977.

L'Engle, Madeline. *Dragons in the Waters*. New York: Farrar, Straus and Giroux, 1976.

———. *A Swiftly Tilting Planet*. New York: Farrar, Straus and Giroux, 1978.

Lightner, A. M. *Star Circus*. New York: E. P. Dutton and Company, 1977.

Little, Jean. *From Anna*. New York: Harper and Row, 1972.

McCaffrey, Anne. *Dragon Song*. New York: Atheneum, 1976.

McGraw, Eloise Jarvis. *Master Cornhill*. New York: Atheneum, 1973.

McHarque, Georgess. *Stoneflight*. New York: Viking Press, 1975.

Miller, Ruth White. *The City Rose*. New York: McGraw-Hill Book Company, 1977.

Moeri, Louise. *A Horse for X, Y, Z*. New York: E. P. Dutton and Company, 1977.

———. *Save Queen of Sheba*. New York: E. P. Dutton, 1981.

Newman, Robert. *The Case of the Baker Street Irregulars*. New York: Atheneum, 1978.

Nostlinger, Christine. *Konrad*. New York: Franklin Watts, 1977.

O'Brien, Robert. *Mrs. Frisby and the Rats of NIMH*. New York: Atheneum, 1971.

O'Dell, Scott. *Sarah Bishop*. Boston: Houghton Mifflin Company, 1980.

Paterson, Katherine. *Bridge to Terabithia*. New York: Thomas Y. Crowell Company, 1977.

———. *The Great Gilly Hopkins*. New York: Thomas Y. Crowell Company, 1978.

Peck, Richard. *Ghosts I Have Been*. New York: Viking Press, 1977.

Peck, Robert Newton. *Patoosie*. New York: Alfred A. Knopf, 1977.

————. *Soup*. New York: Alfred A. Knopf, 1974.

Pfeffer, Susan Beth. *Kid Power*. New York: Franklin Watts, 1977.

Phipson, Joan. *When the City Stopped*. New York: Atheneum, 1978.

Pinkwater, D. Manus. *The Hoboken Chicken Emergency*. Englewood Cliffs, N.J.: Prentice-Hall, 1977.

Pinkwater, Manus. *Wingman*. New York: Dodd, Mead and Company, 1975.

Platt, Kin. *The Ghost of Hellsfire*. New York: Delacorte Press, 1978.

Raskin, Ellen. *The Westing Game*. New York: E. P. Dutton and Company, 1978.

Reiss, Johanna. *The Upstairs Room*. New York: Thomas Y. Crowell Company, 1972.

Roberts, Willo Davis. *The Minden Case*. New York: Atheneum, 1978.

Robertson, Mary Else. *Jeminalee*. New York: McGraw-Hill Book Company, 1977.

Rockwell, Thomas. *How To Eat Fried Worms*. New York: Franklin Watts, 1973.

Rounds, Glen. *Blind Outlaw*. New York: Holiday House, 1980.

Sacks, Marilyn. *Peter and Veronica*. Garden City, N.Y.: Doubleday and Company, 1979.

Sargent, Sarah. *Weird Henry Berg*. New York: Crown Publishers, 1980.

Sebestyen, Quida. *Words by Heart*. Boston: Little, Brown and Company, 1979.

Selfridge, Olive G. *Trouble With Dragons*. Reading, Mass.: Addison-Wesley, 1978.

Showell, Ellen Harvey. *The Ghost of Tillie Jean Cassaway*. New York: Four Winds Press, 1978.

Sivers, Brenda. *The Snailman*. Boston: Little, Brown and Company, 1978.

Skurzynski, Gloria. *What Happened in Hamelin*. New York: Four Winds Presss, 1979.

Sleator, William. *The Green Futures of Tycho*. New York: E. P. Dutton, 1981.

Smith, Emma. *No Way of Telling*. New York: Atheneum, 1972.

Smucker, Barbara. *Runaway to Freedom*. New York: Harper and Row, 1977.

Steig, William. *Abel's Island*. New York: Farrar, Straus, and Giroux, 1976.

Sutcliff, Rosemary. *Sun Horse, Moon Horse*. New York: E. P. Dutton and Company, 1978.

Taylor, Mildred D. *Roll of Thunder, Hear My Cry*. New York: Dial Press, 1976.

————. *Song of the Trees*. New York: Dial Press, 1975.

Taylor, Theodore. *Teetoncey*. Garden City, N.Y.: Doubleday and Company, 1974.

Thiele, Colin. *The Shadow of the Hills*. New York: Harper and Row, 1977.

Westall, Robert. *The Wind Eye*. New York: William Morrow and Company, 1977.

Williams, Ursula Moray. *Bogwoppit*. Nashville: Thomas Nelson, 1978.

Wiseman, David. *Jeremy Visick*. New York: Houghton Mifflin Company, 1981.

Wosmek, Frances. *Never Mind Murder*. Philadelphia: Westminster Press, 1977.

Yep, Lawrence. *Dragon Wings*. New York: Harper and Row, 1975.

————. *Child of the Owl*. New York: Harper and Row, 1977.

Young, Alida E. *Land of the Iron Dragon*. Garden City, N.Y.: Doubleday and Company, 1978.

Appendix M
Picture Books for Older Children

Aardema, Verna. *Bringing the Rain to Kapiti Plain,* illus. Beatriz Vidal. New York: Dial Press, 1981.

――――. *Why Mosquitoes Buzz in People's Ears,* illus. Leo and Diane Dillon. New York: Dial Press, 1975.

Allard, Harry. *Miss Nelson Is Missing!* illus. James Marshall. Boston: Houghton Mifflin Company, 1977.

Anno, Mitsumasa. *The King's Flower.* New York: Collins, 1978.

Baker, Olaf. *Where the Buffaloes Begin,* illus. Stephen Gammell. New York: Frederick Warne, 1981.

Barrett, Judi. *Cloudy With a Chance of Meatballs,* illus. Ron Barrett. New York: Atheneum, 1979.

Baylor, Byrd. *Guess Who My Favorite Person Is,* illus. Robert Andrew Parker. New York: Charles Scribner's Sons, 1977.

――――. *Hawk, I'm Your Brother,* illus. Peter Parnall. New York: Charles Scribner's Sons, 1976.

――――. *They Put on Masks,* illus. Jerry Ingram. New York: Charles Scribner's Sons, 1974.

――――. *The Way To Start a Day,* illus. Peter Parnall. New York: Charles Scribner's Sons, 1978.

――――. *We Walk in Sandy Places,* illus. Marilyn Schweitzer. New York: Charles Scribner's Sons, 1976.

Baylor, Byrd, and Peter Parnall. *The Other Way To Listen.* New York: Charles Scribner's Sons, 1978.

Berson, Harold. *Joseph and the Snake.* New York: Macmillan Publishing Company, 1979.

――――. *Charles and Claudine.* New York: Macmillan Publishing Company, 1980.

Bowden, Joan Chase. *Why the Tides Ebb and Flow,* illus. Marc Brown. Boston: Houghton Mifflin Company, 1979.

Brodsky, Beverly. *Jonah.* Philadelphia: J. B. Lippincott Company, 1977.

Brown, Marcia. *The Blue Jackal.* New York: Charles Scribner's Sons, 1977.

――――. *The Bun.* New York: Harcourt Brace Jovanovich, 1972.

――――. *Felice.* New York: Charles Scribner's Sons, 1958.

――――. *Once a Mouse.* New York: Charles Scribner's Sons, 1961.

Carew, Jan. *The Third Gift,* illus. Leo and Diane Dillon. Boston: Little, Brown and Company, 1974.

Chaffin, Lillie D. *We Be Warm Till Springtime,* illus. Lloyd Bloom. New York: Macmillan Publishing Company, 1980.

Chapman, Carol. *The Tale of Meshka the Kvetch,* illus. Arnold Lobel. New York: E. P. Dutton, 1980.

Christian, Mary Blount. *The Devil Takes You, Barnabas Beane,* illus. Anne Burgess. New York: Thomas Y. Crowell, 1980.

Clark, Ann Nolan. *In the Land of Small Dragon,* illus. Tony Chen. New York: Viking Press, 1979.

Cooney, Barbara. *Chanticleer and the Fox.* New York: Thomas Y. Crowell Company, 1958.

Daughtery, James. *Andy and the Lion.* New York: Viking Press, 1966.

Demi. *Liang and the Magic Paintbrush.* New York: Holt, Rinehart and Winston, 1980.

————. *Under the Shade of the Mulberry Tree.* Englewood Cliffs, N.J.: Prentice-Hall, 1979.

de Paola, Tomie. *The Knight and the Dragon.* New York: G. P. Putnam's Sons, 1980.

de Regniers, Beatrice Schenk. *Little Sister and the Month Brothers,* illus. Margot Tones. New York: Seabury Press, 1976.

Dickerson, Louise. *Good Wife, Good Wife,* illus. Ronald Himler. New York: McGraw-Hill Publishing Company, 1977.

Domanska, Janina. *King Krakus and the Dragon.* New York: William Morrow and Company, 1979.

————. *The Tortoise and the Tree.* New York: William Morrow and Company, 1978.

Farber, Norma. *How the Left-Behind Beasts Built Ararat,* illus. Antonio Frasconi. New York: Walker and Company, 1978.

————. *There Once Was a Woman Who Married a Man,* illus. Lydia Dabcovich. Reading, Mass.: Addison-Wesley, 1978.

Fleischman, Paul. *The Birthday Tree,* illus. Marcia Sewall. New York: Harper and Row, 1979.

Gage, Wilson. *Down in the Boondocks,* illus. Glen Rounds. New York: William Morrow and Company, 1977.

Garrison, Christian. *The Dream Eater,* illus. Diane Goode. Scarsdale, N.Y.: Bradbury Press, 1978.

————. *Little Pieces of the West Wind,* illus. Diane Goode. New York: Bradbury Press, 1975.

George, Jean Craighead. *The Wounded Wolf,* illus. John Schroeder. New York: Harper and Row, 1978.

Ginsburg, Mirra. *The Fisherman's Son,* illus. Tony Chen. New York: Greenwillow Books, 1979.

Goble, Paul. *The Girl Who Loved Wild Horses.* Scarsdale, N.Y.: Bradbury Press, 1978.

Grimm Brothers. *Cinderella,* illus. Svend Otto S. New York: Larousse and Company, 1978.

Haley, Gail. *Go Away, Stay Away.* New York: Charles Scribner's Sons, 1977.

————. *Jack Jouett's Ride.* New York: Viking Press, 1973.

————. *A Story A Story.* New York: Atheneum, 1970.

Hawkesworth, Jenny. *The Lonely Skyscraper,* illus. Emanuel Schongut. Garden City, N.Y.: Doubleday and Company, 1980.

Herman, Charlotte. *On the Way to the Movies,* illus. Diane Dawson. New York: E. P. Dutton, 1980.

Hoban, Russell. *How Tom Beat Captain Najork and His Hired Sportsmen,* illus. Quentin Blake. New York: Atheneum, 1974.

Hogrogian, Nonny. *The Contest.* New York: William Morrow and Company, 1976.

————. *One Fine Day.* New York: Collier Books, 1971.

Horwitz, Elinor Lander. *When the Sky Is Like Lace,* illus. Barbara Cooney. Philadelphia: J. B. Lippincott Company, 1975.

Hutton, Warwick. *The Sleeping Beauty.* New York: Atheneum, 1979.

Isadora, Rachel. *Ben's Trumpet.* New York: William Morrow and Company, 1979.

John, Naomi. *Roadrunner,* illus. Peter and Virginia Parnall. New York: E. P. Dutton, 1980.

Kellogg, Steven. *Pinkerton, Behave!* New York: Dial Press, 1979.

Koenig, Marion. *The Tale of Fancy Nancy.* London: Chatto and Windus, 1977.

Lasker, Joe. *The Strange Voyage of Neptune's Car.* New York: Viking Press, 1977.

Lionni, Leo. *Frederick.* New York: Pantheon Books, 1967.

———. *Geraldine, the Music Mouse.* New York: Pantheon Books, 1979.

———. *Swimmy.* New York: Pantheon Books, 1973.

———. *Tico and the Golden Wings.* New York: Pantheon Books, 1964.

Lobel, Arnold. *How the Rooster Saved the Day,* illus. Anita Lobel. New York: William Morrow and Company, 1977.

———. *The Man Who Took the Indoors Out.* New York: Harper and Row, 1974.

———. *A Treeful of Pigs,* illus. Anita Lobel. New York: William Morrow and Company, 1979.

Macaulay, David. *Castle.* Boston: Houghton Mifflin Company, 1977.

———. *Cathedral.* Boston: Houghton Mifflin Company, 1973.

———. *Pyramid.* Boston: Houghton Mifflin Company, 1975.

Massie, Diane Redfield. *Dazzle.* New York: Parents' Magazine Press, 1969.

McClenathan, Louise. *My Mother Sends Her Wisdom,* illus. Rosekrans Hoffman. New York: William Morrow and Company, 1979.

McCloskey, Robert. *Burt Dow, Deep-Water Man.* New York: Viking Press, 1963.

McDermott, Gerald. *Anansi, the Spider.* New York: Holt, Rinehart and Winston, 1972.

———. *Arrow to the Sun.* New York: Viking Press, 1974.

———. *The Stonecutter.* New York: Viking Press, 1975.

McGovern, Ann. *Mr. Skinner's Skinny House,* illus. Mort Gerber. New York: Four Winds Press, 1980.

Miles, Miska. *Annie and the Old One,* illus. Peter Parnall. Boston: Little Brown and Company, 1971.

Myers, Walter Dean. *The Golden Serpent,* illus. Alice and Martin Provensen. New York: Viking Press, 1980.

Ness, Evaline. *Tom Tit Tot.* New York: Charles Scribner's Sons, 1965.

Nixon, Joan Lowery. *If You Say So, Claude,* illus. Lorinda Bryan Cauley. New York: Frederick Warne, 1980.

Norris, Louanne and Howard E. Smith. *An Oak Tree Dies and a Journey Begins,* illus. Allen Davis. New York: Crown Publishers, 1979.

Paterson, A. B. *Mulga Bill's Bicycle,* illus. Kilmeny andd Deborah Niland. New York: Parent's Magazine Press, 1973.

Pavey, Peter. *I'm Taggarty Toad.* Scarsdale, N.Y.: Bradbury Press, 1980.

Peet, Bill. *The Spooky Tail of Prewitt Peacock.* Boston: Houghton Mifflin Company, 1972.

———. *The Whingdingdilly.* Boston: Houghton Mifflin Company, 1970.

Roach, Marilynne K. *Dune Fox.* Boston: Little Brown and Company, 1977.

Schweitzer, Byrd Baylor. *Amigo,* illus. Garth Williams. New York: Macmillan Publishing Company, 1963.

Scribner, Charles, Jr. *The Devil's Bridge,* illus. Evaline Ness. New York: Charles Scribner's Sons, 1978.

Sharmat, Marjorie. *Gila Monsters Meet You at the Airport,* illus. Bryon Barton. New York: Macmillan Publishing Company, 1980.

Steig, William. *Farmer Palmer's Wagon Ride.* New York: Farrar, Straus and Giroux, 1974.

Stevenson, James. *Could Be Worse.* New York: William Morrow and Company, 1977.

Thayer, Jane. *Applebaum's Have a Robot!* illus. Bari Weissman. New York: William Morrow and Company, 1980.

Thomas, Karen. *The Good Thing the Bad Thing,* illus. Yaroslava. Englewood Cliffs, N.J.: Prentice-Hall, 1979.

Tobias, Tobi. *The Man Who Played Accordian Music,* illus. Nola Langner. New York: Alfred A. Knopf, 1979.

Toye, William. *The Loon's Necklace,* illus. Elizabeth Cleaver. New York: Oxford University Press, 1977.

Van Allsburg, Chris. *The Garden of Abdul Gasazi.* Boston: Houghton Mifflin Company, 1979.

————. *Jumanji.* Boston: Houghton Mifflin Company, 1981.

Waber, Bernard. *You're a Little Kid with a Big Heart.* Boston: Houghton Mifflin Company, 1980.

Wagner, Jenny. *The Bunyip of Berkeley's Creek,* illus. Ron Brooks. Scarsdale, N.Y.: Bradbury Press, 1973.

Ward, Lynd. *The Biggest Bear.* Boston: Houghton Mifflin Company, 1952.

Willard, Nancy. *Simple Pictures Are Best,* illus. Tomie de Paola. New York: Harcourt, Brace and World, 1976.

Williams, Jay. *One Big Wish,* illus. John O'Brien. New York: Macmillan Publishing Company, 1980.

Yarbrough, Camille. *Cornrows,* illus. Carole Byard. New York: Coward, McCann and Geoghegan, 1979.

Yashima, Taro. *Crow Boy.* New York: Viking Press, 1955.

Yolen, Jane. *The Seeing Stick,* illus. Remy Charlip and Demetra Maraslis. New York: Thomas Y. Crowell Company, 1977.

Young, Ed. *The Terrible Nung Gwama.* New York: Collins, 1978.

Zemach, Harve. *The Judge,* illus. Margot Zemach. New York: Farrar, Straus and Giroux, 1969.

Zemach, Harve, and Margot Zemach. *Duffy and the Devil.* New York: Farrar, Straus and Giroux, 1973.

Zemach, Margot. *It Could Always Be Worse.* New York: Farrar, Straus and Giroux, 1976.

Appendix N
Bookmaking Directions

1. Fold paper in half for pages. Diagram A.

2. Sew along dotted lines with needle and thread. (Some teachers are mass-producing all sizes and shapes by using their sewing machines to sew paper.) Diagram B.

3. Cut cloth or wallpaper one inch larger than book pages. Lay open and flat to measure. Diagram C.

4. Cut two pieces of cardboard a little larger than pages. Cardboard from shirts works well. Diagram D.

5. Cut small pieces of drymount to fit between the cardboard pieces and the cloth. Diagram E.

6. Lay cloth flat, place small pieces of drymount on top, then cardboard pieces. Leave space between cardboard pieces to allow book to open and shut. Diagram E.

7. With iron, press a few places to hold cardboard in place.

8. Fold corners over drymount and iron; then fold sides over drymount and iron. Diagram F.

9. Cut two pieces of drymount the same size as open pages. Lay drymount on open cover; then lay open pages on drymount. Press first page and then last page to the cover. Diagram G.

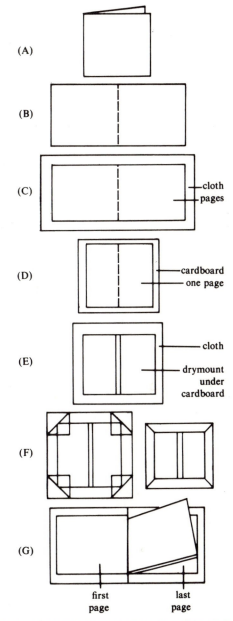

(A)

(B)

(C) — cloth — pages

(D) — cardboard — one page

(E) — cloth — drymount under cardboard

(F)

(G) first page   last page

CAUTION: NEVER PLACE IRON DIRECTLY ON DRY MOUNT BECAUSE IT WILL STICK.

119

Appendix O
Media of Illustrations in Picture Books*

Paint

Watercolor

+Adrienne Adams. *Houses from the Sea,* written by Alice Goudey.
Robert McCloskey. *A Time of Wonder.*
Peter Spier. *London Bridge Is Falling Down* and *Noah's Ark.*
Margot Zemach. *The Judge,* written by Harve Zemach.

Pencil and Watercolor

Marvin Bileck. *Rain Makes Applesauce,* written by Julian Scheer.

Crayon, Ink, and Watercolor

Marcia Brown. *Cinderella.*

Gouache and Poster Paint

Gouache
Roger Duvoisin. *Hide and Seek Fog,* written by Alvin Tresselt.

Poster Paint
Celestino Piatti. *The Holy Night,* written by Aurel von Juchen.

Tempera or Opaque Paint

Maurice Sendak. *Where the Wild Things Are.*
Lynd Ward. *The Silver Pony.*

Acrylics

Ezra Jack Keats. *Dreams.*
Brian Wildsmith. *Brian Wildsmith's ABC.*

Pastels

Nonny Hogrogian. *Always Room for One More,* written by Sorche Nic Leodhas. Also
    pen and ink.

*Further information about illustrators and their media can be found in these volumes:
    Cianciolo, Patricia. *Illustrations in Children's Books.* 2d ed. Dubuque, Iowa: William C. Brown Company
        Publishers, 1976.
    Huck, Charlotte S. *Children's Literature in the Elementary School.* 3d ed. update. New York: Holt,
        Rinehart and Winston, 1979. Chapter 3.
+Unless otherwise noted, the individual listed is both the illustrator and the author.

Crayon

Leo Lionni. *Inch by Inch*. Also felt tip pen.

Graphics

Wood Cuts

Marcia Brown. *Once a Mouse*.
Clement Hurd. *Wingfin and Topple*, written by Evans G. Valens, Jr.
Evaline Ness. *Tom Tit Tot*.

Cardboard Cuts

Blair Lent. *John Tabor's Ride* and *The Wave*, the latter written by Margaret Hodges.

Linoleum Cuts

Marcia Brown. *Dick Whittington and His Cat*.
Gail Haley. *Go Away, Stay Away*.

Wood Engravings

Philip Reed. *Mother Goose and Nursery Rhymes*.

Scratchboard

Barbara Cooney. *Chanticleer and the Fox*.
Serge Prokofieff. *Peter and the Wolf*.

Lithography

Stone: Edgar and Ingri D'Aulaire. *Abraham Lincoln*.
Zinc: Robert McCloskey. *Make Way for Ducklings*.

Collage and Multi-Media

Ezra Jack Keats. *The Snowy Day, Jennie's Hat*, and many other books.
Leo Lionni. *Inch by Inch, Frederick, Little Blue and Little Yellow, Swimmy*.

Photography

Marcia Brown. *Listen to a Shape, Touch Will Tell*, and *Walk With Your Eyes*.
Tana Hoban. *Look Again*.
Albert Lamorisse. *The Red Balloon*.

Appendix P
Library References of Children's Books*

General

> *Children's Catalog*
> H.H. Wilson

Factual Material

> *The A.A.A.'s Science Book List for Children.* American Association for the Advancement of Science, 1972.
>
> Mattias, Margaret
> *Children's Mathematics Books*
> A.L.A., 1979.

Picture Books

> *Younkers Public Library Children's Services*
> Ocena Publications, 1979.

Folklore

> Ireland, Norma Olin
> *Index to Fairy Tales*
> F.W. Faxon Company

Poetry

> Brewton, John
> *Index to Children's Poetry*
> H.W. Wilson
>
> Smith, Dorothy
> *Subject Index to Poetry for Children and Young People: 1957–1975*
> A.L.A.
>
> *Subject Index to Children's Magazines*
> (a source of poetry, especially on holiday themes)

*Lucille Lettow, Youth Librarian, and Arlene Ruthenberg, Emeritus Youth Librarian, University of Northern Iowa, provided information for this appendix.

Concepts and Themes

Dreyer, Sharon

The Bookfinder

Literature about needs and problems of children and youth, ages 2–15.

Fassler, Joan

Helping Children Cope

Free Press, 1978.

Literature for children, ages 4–8, on potentially stressful aspects of living.

Gillespie, John T.

Best Book for Children: Preschool Through the Middle Grades.

R.R. Bowker, 1978.

Literature for various curriculum areas.

Gillis, Ruth J.

Children's Books for Times of Stress

Indiana University Press, 1978.

Literature for concepts related to social-emotional development.

Subject Index to Children's Magazines

Literature for holidays.

Appendix Q
The Loner

EXTERNAL RESPONSES

Giving of People to David

Migrant workers desert him when he is ill.	The girl, Raidy, befriends him because he is alone. She is killed.	Boss, the ranch woman, offers him a home. Tex relates that the boy and Boss may be like an orphan lamb and an old ewe.	Tex tries to show him that being a loner is a selfish lifestyle.	Angie gives friendship and believes in him. She reminds him of Raidy. Angie tutors him.	Boss wants him to live up to his name and to her son, Ben. She teaches him responsibility and respect for the lives of others through shepherding.	Tex shows David how to use gun and to hunt grizzlies. Boss gives Ben's gun to David for Christmas.

SEARCH FOR IDENTITY

Code of living: One should look out for oneself rather than for others.

The boy does not blame migrant workers because they must look after themselves.	He wanders blindly after her tragic death and is found by a ranch woman in Montana.	He accepts Boss' offer of home. Winter is coming so going to California is unwise at this time. He finds a name for himself— David.	At first David attempts to escape, but he is found by Boss and dog. By looking for David, they have left the flock open to attack by coyotes. The dog, Jup, is injured trying to protect flock. David stays to help Boss because he feels guilty. He takes care of the injured dog.		David begins to become a part of the world of shepherding but makes many mistakes. His false signals cause sheep to panic. He allows Jup to be blamed. He saves Jup from being mistakenly shot for rabies.	David renews his effort to help in shepherding.

David Giving to People

INTERNAL RESPONSES

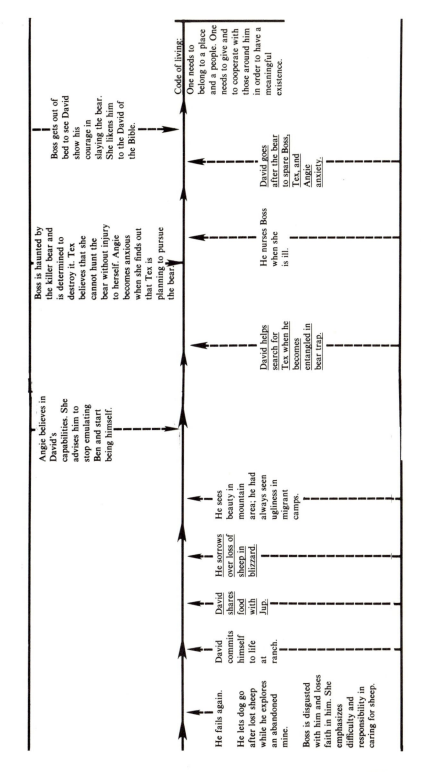

He fails again.

He lets dog go after lost sheep while he explores an abandoned mine.

Boss is disgusted with him and loses faith in him. She emphasizes difficulty and responsibility in caring for sheep.

David commits himself to life at ranch.

David shares food with Jup.

He sorrows over loss of sheep in blizzard.

He sees beauty in mountain area; he had always seen ugliness in migrant camps.

Angie believes in David's capabilities. She advises him to stop emulating Ben and start being himself.

David helps search for Tex when he becomes entangled in bear trap.

Boss is haunted by the killer bear and is determined to destroy it. Tex believes that she cannot hunt the bear without injury to herself. Angie becomes anxious when she finds out that Tex is planning to pursue the bear.

He nurses Boss when she is ill.

David goes after the bear to spare Boss, Tex, and Angie anxiety.

Boss gets out of bed to see David show his courage in slaying the bear. She likens him to the David of the Bible.

Code of living:
One needs to belong to a place and a people. One needs to give and to cooperate with those around him in order to have a meaningful existence.

Appendix R
Literature for Children in Grades Two and Three*

Aardema, Verna. *Bringing the Rain to Kapiti Plain,* illus. Beatriz Vidal. New York: Dial Press, 1981.

———. *Why Mosquitoes Buzz in People's Ears,* illus. Leo and Diane Dillon. New York: Dial Press, 1975.

Alexander, Sue. *Marc the Magnificent,* illus. Tomie de Paola. New York: Pantheon Books, 1978.

Allard, Harry. *Bumps in the Night,* illus. James Marshall. Garden City, N.Y.: Doubleday and Company, 1979.

———. *Miss Nelson Is Missing,* illus. James Marshall. Boston: Houghton Mifflin Company, 1977.

Allen, Linda. *Lionel and the Spy Next Door.* New York: William Morrow and Company, 1980.

———. *Mrs. Simkin's Bed,* illus. Loretta Lustig. New York: William Morrow and Company, 1980.

Annett, Cora. *How the Witch Got Alf,* illus. Steven Kellogg. New York: Franklin Watts, 1975.

Anno, Mitsumasa. *The King's Flower.* New York: Collins, 1978.

Bach, Alice. *The Most Delicious Camping Trip Ever,* illus. Steven Kellogg. New York: Harper and Row, 1976.

Balian, Lorna. *Leprechauns Never Die.* Nashville: Abingdon, 1980.

Bang, Betsy. *The Cucumber Stem,* illus. Tony Chen. New York: Greenwillow Books, 1980.

Barrett, Judi. *Animals Should Definitely "Not" Act Like People,* illus. Ron Barrett. New York: Atheneum, 1980.

———. *Cloudy with a Chance of Meatballs,* illus. Ron Barrett. New York: Atheneum, 1979.

Bason, Lillian. *Those Foolish Molboes.* New York: Coward, McCann and Geoghegan, 1973.

Baylor, Byrd. *Guess Who My Favorite Person Is,* illus. Robert Andrew Parker. New York: Charles Scribner's Sons, 1977.

Berson, Harold. *Joseph and the Snake.* New York: Macmillan Publishing Company, 1979.

———. *Charles and Claudine.* New York: Macmillan Publishing Company, 1980.

Blood, Charles L., and Martin Link. *The Goat in the Rug.* New York: Parents' Magazine Press, 1976.

Bonners, Susan. *Panda.* New York: Delacorte Press, 1978.

Brady, Irene. *Doodlebug.* Boston: Houghton Mifflin Company, 1977.

Brandenberg, Franz. *What Can You Make of It?* New York: William Morrow and Company, 1977.

*Most books can be used with a wide range of ages. The author chose to make a special list for children in grades two and three because the needs of this group of children often are overlooked.

Brett, Jan. *Fritz and the Beautiful Horses.* Boston: Houghton Mifflin Company, 1981.

Brittain, Bill. *The Devil's Donkey,* illus. Andrew Glass. New York: Harper and Row, 1981.

Brown, Marc. *The True Franchine.* Boston: Little, Brown and Company, 1981.

Brown, Marcia. *The Blue Jackal.* New York: Charles Scribner's Sons, 1977.

——— . *The Bun.* New York: Harcourt Brace Jovanovich, 1972.

——— . *Once a Mouse.* New York: Charles Scribner's Sons, 1961.

Brown, Margaret Wise. *Fox Eyes,* illus. Garth Williams. New York: Pantheon Books, 1977.

Bunting, Eve. *The Big Cheese.* New York: Macmillan Publishing Company, 1977.

Burningham, John. *Would You Rather . . .* New York: Thomas Y. Crowell Company, 1978.

Byars, Betsy. *After the Goat Man.* New York: Viking Press, 1974.

Calhoun, Mary. *The Witch Who Lost Her Shadow,* illus. Trinka Hakes Noble. New York: Harper and Row, 1979.

Carlson, Natalie Savage. *Runaway Marie Louise,* illus. Jose Aruego and Ariane Dewey. New York: Charles Scribner's Sons, 1977.

Carrick, Carol. *The Accident.* New York: Seabury Press, 1976.

Carrick, Malcolm. *Happy Jack.* New York: Harper and Row, 1979.

Chaffin, Lillie D. *We Be Warm Till Springtime Comes,* illus. Lloyd Bloom. New York: Macmillan Publishing Company, 1980.

Chapman, Carol. *The Tale of Meshka the Kvetch,* illus. Arnold Lobel. New York: E.P. Dutton, 1980.

Christian, Mary Blount. *The Lucky Man,* illus. Glen Rounds. New York: Macmillan Publishing Company, 1979.

——— . *The Devil Take You, Barnabas Beane,* illus. Anne Burgess. New York: Thomas Y. Crowell, 1980.

Cleary, Beverly. *Ramona and Her Father.* New York: William Morrow and Company, 1977.

——— . *Ramona the Brave.* New York: William Morrow and Company, 1975.

Clifton, Lucille. *The Lucky Stone,* illus. Dale Payson. New York: Delacorte Press, 1979.

Coombs, Patricia. *The Magic Pot.* New York: Lothrop, Lee and Shephard, 1977.

Coren, Alan. *Arthur the Kid.* Boston: Little, Brown and Company, 1977.

Craft, Ruth, and Irene Haas. *Carrie Hepple's Garden.* New York: Atheneum, 1979.

Craig, M. Jean. *The Donkey Prince,* illus. Barbara Cooney. New York: Doubleday and Company, 1977.

Daly, Niki. *Vim the Rag Mouse.* New York: Atheneum, 1979.

Delton, Judy. *Kitty in the Middle.* New York: Houghton Mifflin and Company, 1979.

——— . *Penny-Wise, Fun-Foolish,* illus. Giulio Maestro. New York: Crown Publishers, 1977.

Demi. *Liang and the Magic Paintbrush.* New York: Holt, Rinehart and Winston, 1980.

——— . *Under the Shade of the Mulberry Tree.* Englewood Cliffs, N.J.: Prentice-Hall, 1979.

de Paola, Tomie. *The Knight and the Dragon.* New York: G.P. Putnam's Sons, 1980.

——— . *The Quicksand Book.* New York: Holiday House, 1977.

Domanska, Janina. *King Krakus and the Dragon.* New York: William Morrow and Company, 1979.

Duff, Maggie. *Rum Pum Pum,* illus. Jose Aruego and Ariane Dewey. New York: Macmillan Publishing Company, 1978.

Duvoisin, Roger. *Jasmine.* New York: Alfred A. Knopf, 1973.

———. *Petunia.* New York: Alfred A. Knopf, 1950.

Erickson, Russell E. *A Toad for Tuesday.* New York: Lothrop, Lee, and Shephard, 1974.

Evans, Mari. *Jim Flying High,* illus. Ashley Brayan. Garden City, N.Y.: Doubleday and Company, 1979.

Firmin, Peter. *Basil Brush Builds a House.* Englewood Cliffs, N.J.: Prentice-Hall, 1977.

Fleischman, Paul. *The Birthday Tree,* illus. Marcia Sewell. New York: Harper and Row, 1979.

Fleischman, Sid. *McBroan and the Great Race.* Boston: Little, Brown and Company, 1980.

Foley, Louise Munro. *Tackle 22,* illus. John Heinly. New York: Delacorte Press, 1978.

Freemore, Don. *Bearymore.* New York: Viking Press, 1976.

———. *Dandelion.* New York: Viking Press, 1964.

Gage, Wilson. *Down in the Boondocks,* illus. Glen Rounds. New York: William Morrow and Company, 1977.

Galdone, Joanna. *Little Girl and the Big Bear,* illus. Paul Galdone. New York: Houghton Mifflin, 1981.

Galdone, Paul. *Cinderella.* New York: McGraw-Hill Book Company, 1978.

———. *Henny Penny.* New York: Seabury Press, 1968.

———. *The History of Mother Twaddle.* New York: Seabury Press, 1974.

———. *King of Cats.* New York: Houghton Mifflin, 1980.

———. *The Little Red Hen.* New York: Seabury Press, 1973.

———. *Puss in Boots.* New York: Seabury Press, 1976.

Gantos, Jack. *Rotten Ralph,* illus. Nicole Rubel. Boston: Houghton Mifflin Company, 1976.

Gantos, Jack and Micole Rubel. *The Perfect Pal.* Boston: Houghton Mifflin Company, 1979.

Garrison, Christian. *The Dream Eater,* illus. Diane Goode. Scarsdale, N.Y.: Bradbury Press, 1978.

———. *Little Pieces of the West Wind,* illus. Diane Goode. Scarsdale, N.Y.: Bradbury Press, 1975.

Gauch, Patricia Lee. *This Time, Tempe Wick?* New York: Coward, McCann and Geoghegan, 1974.

Gelman, Rita Golden and Joan Richter. *Professor Coconut and the Thief.* New York: Holt, Rinehart and Winston, 1977.

George, Jean Craighead. *The Wentletrap Trap,* illus. Symeon Shimin. New York: E.P. Dutton and Company, 1978.

Ginsburg, Mirra. *The Fisherman's Sons,* illus. Tony Chen. New York: Greenwillow Books, 1979.

Greenfield, Eloise. *She Came Bringing Me That Little Baby Girl,* illus. John Steptoe. Philadelphia: J.B. Lippincott Company, 1974.

Greenwald, Sheila. *Give Us a Great Big Smile, Rosy Cole.* Boston: Little, Brown and Company, 1981.

Grimm Brothers. *The Seven Ravens,* illus. Lisabeth Zwerger. New York: William Morrow, 1981.

Haley, Gail E. *Go Away, Stay Away.* New York: Charles Scribner's Sons, 1977.

Hall, Malcolm. *Headlines.* New York: Coward, McCann and Geoghegan, 1973.

Hanlon, Emily. *How a Horse Grew Hoarse on the Site Where He Sighted a Bare Bear.* New York: Delacorte Press, 1976.

Hatch, Shirley Cook. *Wind Is To Feel.* New York: Coward, McCann and Geoghegan, 1973.

Hawkesworth, Jenny. *The Lonely Skyscraper,* illus. Emanuel Schongut. Garden City, N.Y.: Doubleday Company, 1980.

Hazen, Barbara Shook. *Step On It, Andrew,* illus. Lisl Weil. New York: Atheneum, 1980.

Heine, Helme. *Mr. Miller the Dog.* New York: Atheneum, 1980.

Herman, Charlotte. *On the Way to the Movies,* illus. Diane Dawson. New York: E.P. Dutton, 1980.

Hoban, Lillian. *Here Come Raccoons.* New York: Holt, Rinehart and Winston, 1977.

Hoban, Russell. *How Tom Beat Captain Najork and His Hired Sportsmen,* illus. Quentin Blake. New York: Atheneum, 1974.

Hodges, Margaret. *The Little Humpbacked Horse,* illus. Chris Conover. New York: Farrar, Straus and Giroux, 1980.

Hogrogian, Nonny. *Carrot Cake.* New York: William Morrow and Company, 1977.

———— . *Cinderella.* New York: Greenwillow Books, 1981.

———— . *The Contest.* New York: William Morrow and Company, 1976.

———— . *One Fine Day.* New York: Collier Books, 1971.

Horwitz, Elinor Lander. *When the Sky Is Like Lace,* illus. Barbara Cooney. Philadelphia: J.B. Lippincott Company, 1975.

Howe, Deborah and James. *Teddy Bear's Scrapbook.* New York: Atheneum, 1980.

Hutchins, Pat. *Follow That Bus!* New York: William Morrow and Company, 1977.

———— . *Rosie's Walk.* New York: Macmillan Publishing Company, 1968.

Inkiow, Dimiter. *Me and My Sister Clara.* New York: Pantheon Books, 1979.

Jeschke, Susan. *Sidney.* New York: Holt, Rinehart and Winston, 1975.

Kahl, Virginia. *Whose Cat Is That?* New York: Charles Scribner's Sons, 1979.

Keats, Ezra Jack. *Goggles.* New York: Macmillan Publishing Company, 1969.

———— . *Hi, Cat!* New York: Macmillan Publishing Company, 1970.

———— . *Pet Show.* New York: Macmillan Publishing Company, 1972.

Kellogg, Steven. *The Mysterious Tadpole.* New York: Dial Press, 1977.

———— . *Pinkerton, Behave!* New York: Dial Press, 1979.

Kennedy, Richard. *The Porcelain Man,* illus. Marcia Sewall. Boston: Little, Brown and Company, 1976.

Kent, Jack. *Hoddy Doddy.* New York: William Morrow and Company, 1979.

———— . *There's No Such Thing as a Dragon.* New York: Golden Press, 1975.

Koenig, Marion. *The Tale of Fancy Nancy.* London: Chatto and Windus, 1977.

Kraus, Robert. *Owliver,* illus. Jose Aruego and Ariane Dewey. New York: E.P. Dutton and Company, 1974.

———— . *Leo the Late Bloomer,* illus. Jose Aruego. New York: Windmill Books, 1971.

Kroll, Steven. *The Tyrannosaurus Game,* illus. Tomie de Paola. New York: Holiday House, 1976.

Leny, Elizabeth. *Frankenstein Moved in on the Fourth Floor.* New York: Harper and Row, 1979.

Levitin, Sonia. *Nobody Stole the Pig,* illus. Fernando. New York: Harcourt Brace Jovanovich, 1980.

Lewis, Thoma P. *Call Me Mr. Sniff,* illus. Beth Weiner Woldin. New York: Harper and Row, 1981.

———— . *The Dragon Kite.* New York: Holt, Rinehart and Winston, 1974.

Lionni, Leo. *Frederick.* New York: Pantheon Books, 1967.

———— . *Inch by Inch.* New York: Astor, 1960.

———— . *I Want to Stay Here! I Want to Go There!* New York: Pantheon Books, 1977.

Lisowski, Gabriel. *How Tevye Became a Milkman.* New York: Holt, Rinehart and Winston, 1976.

Lively, Penelope. *Fanny's Sister.* New York: E.P. Dutton, 1976.

Lobel, Arnold. *How the Rooster Saved the Day,* illus. Anita Lobel. New York: William Morrow and Company, 1977.

———— . *The Man Who Took the Indoors Out.* New York: Harper and Row, 1974.

———— . *A Treeful of Pigs,* illus. Anita Lobel. New York: William Morrow and Company, 1979.

Mack, Gail. *Yesterday's Snowman,* illus. Erick Blegvad. New York: Pantheon Books, 1979.

Maitland, Anthony. *Idle Jack.* New York: Farrar, Straus and Giroux, 1977.

Massie, Diane Redfield. *Dazzle.* New York: Parents' Magazine Press, 1969.

Mayer, Mercer. *Mrs. Beggs and the Wizard.* New York: Parents' Magazine Press, 1973.

McClenathan, Louise. *My Mother Sends Her Wisdom,* illus. Rosekrans Hoffman. New York: William Morrow and Company, 1979.

McClure, Gillian. *Fly Home Mc Doo.* London: Andre Deutsch, 1979.

McPhail, David. *Grandfather's Cake.* New York: Charles Scribner's Sons, 1979.

Miles, Miska. *Annie and the Old One,* illus. Peter Parnall. Boston: Little, Brown and Company, 1971.

———— . *Chicken Forgets,* illus. Jim Arnosky. Boston: Little, Brown and Company, 1976.

———— . *Somebody's Dog.* illus. John Schoenherr. Boston: Little, Brown and Company, 1973.

———— . *Swim, Little Duck,* illus. Jim Arnosky. Boston: Little, Brown and Company, 1976.

Molarsky, Osmond. *The Peasant and the Fly.* New York: Harcourt Brace Jovanovich, 1980.

Mosel, Arlene. *The Funny Little Woman,* illus. Blair Lent. New York: E.P. Dutton and Company, 1972.

Noble, Trinka Hakes. *The Day Jimmy's Boa Ate the Wash,* illus. Steven Kellogg. New York: Dial Press, 1980.

Pavey, Peter. *I'm Taggerty Toad.* Scarsdale, N.Y.: Bradbury Press, 1980.

Peet, Bill. *Big Bad Bruce.* Boston: Houghton, Mifflin and Company, 1977.

———— . *Merle the High Flying Squirrel.* Boston: Houghton Mifflin Company, 1974.

———— . *The Spooky Tail of Prewitt Peacock.* Boston: Houghton Mifflin Company, 1972.

———— . *The Whingdingdilly.* Boston: Houghton Mifflin Company, 1970.

Robinson, Nancy K. *Wendy and the Bullies*. New York: Hastings House, 1980.

Roffey, Maureen and Bernard Lodge. *Rhyming Nell*. New York: Lothrop, Lee and Shephard, 1979.

Ruchlis, Hy. *How a Rock Came To Be in a Fence in a Road Near a Town*. New York: Walker and Company, 1973.

Ryan, Cheli Duran. *Hildilid's Night,* illus. Arnold Lobel. New York: Macmillan Publishing Company, 1971.

Sharmat, Marjorie. *Gila Monsters Meet You at the Airport,* illus. Bryan Barton. New York: Macmillan Publishing Company, 1980.

———— . *Griselda's New Year,* illus. Normand Chartier. New York: Macmillan Publishing Company, 1979.

Sharmont, Marjorie Weinman & Mitchell Sharmont. *The Day I Was Born,* illus. Diane Dawson. New York: E.P. Dutton, 1980.

———— . *I Am Not a Pest,* illus. Diane Dawson. New York: E.P. Dutton and Company, 1979.

Sleator, William. *Once, Said Darlene,* illus. Steven Kellogg. New York: E.P. Dutton and Company, 1979.

Sortor, Toni. *Adventures of B.J.* Nashville: Abingdon, 1975.

Steig, William. *The Amazing Bone*. New York: Farrar, Straus and Giroux, 1976.

———— . *Caleb and Kate*. New York: Farrar, Straus and Giroux, 1977.

———— . *Farmer Palmer's Wagon Ride*. New York: Farrar, Straus and Giroux, 1974.

Stern, Simon. *The Hobyahs*. Englewood Cliffs, N.J.: Prentice-Hall, 1977.

Stevens, Carla. *Pig and the Blue Flag*. New York: Seabury Press, 1977.

———— . *Stories From a Snowy Meadow*. New York: Four Winds Press, 1976.

Stevenson, James. *Could Be Worse*. New York: William Morrow and Company, 1977.

———— . *Wilfred the Rat*. New York: William Morrow and Company, 1977.

Tether, Graham. *Skunk and Possum,* illus. Lucinda McQueen. Boston: Houghton Mifflin Company, 1979.

Thayer, Jane. *Applebaum's Have a Robot!* illus. Bari Weissman. New York: William Morrow and Company, 1980.

Thomas, Ianthe. *Willie Blows a Mean Horn,* illus. Ann Toulmin. New York: Harper and Row, 1981.

Thomas, Jane Resh. *Elizabeth Catches a Fish*. New York: Seabury Press, 1977.

Thomas, Karen. *The Good Thing the Bad Thing,* illus. Yaroslava. Englewood Cliffs, N.J.: Prentice-Hall, 1979.

Tresselt, Alvin. *What Did You Leave Behind?* illus. Roger Duvoisin. New York: Lothrop, Lee and Shephard, 1978.

Turpin, Lorna. *The Sultan's Snakes*. New York: Greenwillow Books, 1979.

Valen, Nanine. *The Devil's Tale*. New York: Charles Scribner's Sons, 1978.

Van Allsburg, Chris. *The Garden of Abdul Gasazi*. Boston: Houghton Mifflin Company, 1979.

———— . *Jumanji*. Boston: Houghton Mifflin Company, 1981.

Viorst, Judith. *Alexander Who Used To Be Rich Last Sunday,* illus. Ray Cruz. New York: Atheneum, 1978.

Vogel, Ilse-Margaret. *Dodo Every Day*. New York: Harper and Row, 1977.

Waber, Bernard. *Mice on My Mind*. Boston: Houghton Mifflin Company, 1976.

——— . *You're a Little Kid with a Big Heart*. Boston: Houghton Mifflin Company, 1980.

——— . *"You Look Ridiculous," Said the Rhinoceros to the Hippopotamus*. Boston: Houghton Mifflin Company, 1966.

Wahl, Jan. *Dracula's Cat,* illus. Kay Chorao. Englewood Cliffs, N.J.: Prentice-Hall, 1978.

Walker, Barbara. *Teeny-Tiny and the Witch-Woman,* illus. Michael Foreman. New York: Pantheon Books, 1975.

Wallace, Barbara Brooks. *Palmer Patch*. Chicago: Follett Publishing Company, 1976.

Wells, Rosemary. *Abdul*. New York: Dial Press, 1975.

——— . *Benjamin and Tulip*. New York: Dial Press, 1973.

——— . *Unfortunately Harriet*. New York: Dial Press, 1972.

Willard, Nancy. *Simple Pictures Are Best,* illus. Tomie de Paola. New York: Harcourt, Brace and World, 1976.

Williams, Jay. *One Big Wish,* illus. John O'Brien. New York: Macmillan Publishing Company, 1980.

Yarbough, Camille. *Cornrows,* illus. Carole Byard. New York: Coward, McCann and Geoghegan, 1979.

Yolen, Jane. *The Seeing Stick,* illus. Remy Charlip and Demetra Maraslis. New York: Thomas Y. Crowell Company, 1977.

——— . *Commander Toad in Space,* illus. Bruce Degen. New York: Coward, McCann and Geoghegan, 1980.

Young, Ed. *The Terrible Nung Gwama*. New York: Collins, 1978.

Zemach, Harve. *The Judge,* illus. Margot Zemach. New York: Farrar, Straus and Giroux, 1969.

Zemach, Harve and Margot Zemach. *Duffy and the Devil*. New York: Farrar, Straus and Giroux, 1973.

Zemach, Kaethe. *The Beautiful Rat*. New York: Four Winds Press, 1979.

Zemach, Margot. *It Could Always Be Worse*. New York: Farrar, Straus and Giroux, 1976.

Appendix S
Recent Books for Discussion
in Junior High School

Realism

Appel, Benjamin. *Hell's Kitchen*. New York: Pantheon Books, 1977.

Avi. *A Place Called Ugly*. New York: Pantheon Books, 1981.

Ballard, Martin. *Dockie*. New York: Harper and Row, 1972.

Barford, Carol. *Let Me Hear the Music*. New York: Seabury Press, 1979.

Branscum, Robbie. *To the Tune of a Hickory House*. Garden City, N.Y.: Doubleday and Company, 1978.

Budbill, David. *Bones on Black Spruce Mountain*. New York: Dial Press, 1978.

Bunting, Eve. *Blackbird Singing*. New York: Macmillan Publishing Company, 1980.

Burch, Robert. *Wilkin's Ghost*. New York: Viking Press, 1978.

Byars, Betsy. *Good-Bye Chicken Little*. New York: Harper and Row, 1979.

——— . *The Pinballs*. New York: Harper and Row, 1977.

Callen, Larry. *The Deadly Mandrake*. Boston: Little, Brown and Company, 1978.

Carter, Peter. *Under Goliath*. Oxford: Oxford University Press, 1977.

Conford, Ellen. *Dear Lovely Heart, I Am Desperate*. Boston: Little Brown and Company, 1975.

Cummings, Betty Sue. *Let a River Be*. New York: Atheneum, 1978.

Cunningham, Julia. *Come to the Edge*. New York: Pantheon Books, 1977.

——— . *Tuppeny*. New York: E. P. Dutton and Company, 1978.

Degens, T. *The Game of Thatcher Island*. New York: Viking Press, 1977.

Edmonds, Walter D. *Bert Breen's Barn*. Boston: Little, Brown and Company, 1975.

Fenton, Edward. *Duffy's Rocks*. New York: E.P. Dutton and Company, 1974.

Forman, James. *A Fine, Soft Day*. New York: Farrar, Straus and Giroux, 1978.

Gerson, Corinne. *Passing Through*. New York: Dial Press, 1978.

Griffiths, Helen. *Running Wild*. New York: Holiday House, 1977.

Grohskapf, Bernice. *Children in the Wind*. New York: Atheneum, 1977.

Hale, Nancy. *The Night of the Hurricane*. New York: Coward, McCann and Geoghegan, 1978.

Leitch, Patricia. *The Fields of Praise*. Philadelphia: J.B. Lippincott Company, 1975.

McCord, Jean. *Turkeylegs Thompson*. New York: Atheneum, 1979.

Miles, Betty. *Maudie and Me and the Dirty Book*. New York: Alfred A. Knopf, 1980.

Paterson, Katherine. *The Great Gilly Hopkins*. New York: Thomas Y. Crowell Company, 1978.

Peck, Richard. *Father Figure*. New York: Viking Press, 1978.

Phipson, Joan. *Fly Into Danger*. New York: Atheneum, 1977.

——— . *When the City Stopped*. New York: Atheneum, 1978.

Rabe, Berniece. *The Girl Who Had No Name*. New York: E.P. Dutton and Company, 1977.
Shura, Mary Francis. *The Season of Silence*. New York: Atheneum, 1976.
Sivers, Brenda. *The Snailman*. Boston: Little, Brown and Company, 1977.
Thiele, Colin. *The Shadow on the Hills*. New York: Harper and Row, 1977.

Handicaps

Beckman, Delores. *My Own Private Sky*. New York: E.P. Dutton, 1980. (Small size and crippled)
Byars, Betsy. *The House of Wings*. New York: Viking Press, 1972. (Mental retardation)
Cunningham, Julia. *Burnish Me Bright*. New York: Pantheon Books, 1970. (Deafness)
Kerr, M. E. *Little Little*. New York: Harper and Row, 1981. (Diminutive size)
Little, Jean. *From Anna*. New York: Harper and Row, 1972. (Learning problems and sight)
Naylor, Phyllis Reynolds. *Shadows on the Wall*. New York: Atheneum, 1980. (Huntington's disease)
Slepian, Jan. *The Alfred Summer*. New York: Macmillan Publishing Company, 1980. (Mental retardation and cerebral palsy)
Sutcliff, Rosemary. *Witch's Brat*. New York: Henry Z. Walck, 1970. (Crippled)

Socio-Emotional Problems

Escaping Reality

Arthur, Ruth M. *Miss Ghost*. New York: Atheneum, 1979.
Byars, Betsy. *The Cartoonist*. New York: Viking Press, 1978.
Davies, Andrew. *Conrad's War*. New York: Crown Publishers, 1980.
Lutters, Valeria A. *The Haunting of Julia Unger*. New York: Atheneum, 1977.
McGraw, Eloise Jarvis. *A Really Weird Summer*. New York: Atheneum, 1977.

Death

Jansson, Tove. *The Summer Book*. New York: Random House, 1974.
Lowry, Lois. *A Summer To Die*. Boston: Houghton Mifflin and Company, 1977.

Old Age

Burch, Robert. *Two That Were Tough*. New York: Viking Press, 1976.
Mazer, Norma Fox. *A Figure of Speech*. New York: Delacorte Press, 1973.
Pollowitz, Melinda. *Cinnamon Game*. New York: Harper and Row, 1977.

Foster Children

Byars, Betsy. *The Pinballs*. New York: Harper and Row, 1977.
Paterson, Katherine. *The Great Gilly Hopkins*. New York: Thomas Y. Crowell Company, 1978.

Family in Transition

Allen, Mabel Esther. *Bridge of Friendship*. New York: Dodd, Mead and Company, 1975.
Madison, Winifred. *Call Me Danica*. New York: Four Winds Press, 1977.
Murphy, Barbara Beasley. *No Place To Run*. New York: Bradbury Press, 1977.
Yep, Laurence. *Owl in the Family*. New York: Harper and Row, 1977.

Sexism—Society Predetermining Role of Girls and Women

Branscum, Robbie. *Johnny May*. Garden City, N.Y.: Doubleday and Company, 1975.
Lampman, Evelyn Sibley. *Bargain Bride*. New York: Atheneum, 1977.
Rabe, Berniece. *Naomi*. Nashville: Thomas Nelson, 1975.
Thrasher, Crystal. *The Dark Didn't Catch Me*. New York: Atheneum, 1975.
Willard, Barbara. *The Lark and the Laurel*. New York: Harcourt, Brace, and World, 1970.

Cultural, Ethnic, Racial

Carter, Forrest. *The Education of Little Tree*. New York: Delacorte Press, 1976. (American Indian)
Crowley, Jay. *The Silent One*. New York: Alfred A. Knopf, 1981. (South Seas)
George, Jean Craighead. *Julie of the Wolves*. New York: Harper and Row, 1972. (Eskimo)
Hassler, Jon. *Jemmy*. New York: Atheneum, 1980. (American Indian—White)
Hightower, Jamake. *Anpao*. Philadelphia: J.B. Lippincott Company, 1977. (American Indian)
Levoy, Myron. *Alan and Naomi*. New York: Harper and Row, 1977. (Jewish)
Mohr, Nicholasa. *In Nueva York*. New York: Dial Press, 1977. (Puerto Rican)
Roy, Thomas. *The Curse of the Turtle*. New York: Collins, 1978. (Australian Aborigine)
Sebestyen, Ouida. *Words by Heart*. Boston: Little, Brown and Company, 1979. (Black)
Taylor, Mildred D. *Roll of Thunder, Hear My Cry*. New York: Dial Press, 1976. (Black)
Yep, Lawrence. *Child of the Owl*. New York: Harper and Row, 1977. (Chinese-American)

Historical Fiction

Bell, Frederic. *Jenny's Corner*. New York: Random House, 1974.
Bickham, Jack M. *Dinah, Blow Your Horn*. Garden City, N.Y.: Doubleday and Company, 1979.
Briggs, K. M. *Kate Crackernuts*. New York: Greenwillow Books, 1979.

Burchard, Peter. *The Deserter*. New York: Coward, McCann and Geoghegan, 1973.

———— . *Digger*. New York: G. P. Putnam's Sons, 1980.

———— . *Whaleboat Raid*. New York: Coward, McCann and Geoghegan, 1977.

Burton, Hester. *To Ravensrigg*. New York: Thomas Y. Crowell Company, 1977.

Calvert, Patricia. *Snowbird*. New York: Charles Scribner's Sons, 1980.

Cheatham, K. Follis. *Bring Home the Ghost*. New York: Harcourt Brace Jovanovich, 1980.

Clifford, Eth. *The Curse of the Moonraker*. Boston: Houghton-Mifflin Company, 1977.

Cummings, Betsy Sue. *Hew Against the Grain*. New York: Atheneum, 1977.

Dank, Milton, *Khaki Wings*. New York: Delacorte Press, 1980.

Finlayson, Ann. *The Silver Bullet*. Nashville: Thomas Nelson, 1978.

Haugaard, Erik. *Cromwell's Boy*. Boston: Houghton Mifflin Company, 1978.

Keith, Harold. *The Obstinate Land*. New York: Thomas Y. Crowell Company, 1971.

Miles, Patricia. *Nobody's Child*. New York: E.P. Dutton and Company, 1975.

Moeri, Louise. *Save Queen of Sheba*. New York: E.P. Dutton, 1981.

Peck, Robert Newton. *Fawn*. Boston: Little, Brown and Company, 1975.

———— . *Justice Lion*. Boston: Little, Brown and Company, 1981.

———— . *Rabbits and Redcoats*. New York: Walker and Company, 1976.

St. George, Judith. *The Halo Wind*. New York: G.P. Putnam's Sons, 1978.

Sutcliff Rosemary. *Bloodfeud*. New York: E.P. Dutton and Company, 1976.

———— . *Sun Horse, Moon Horse*. New York: E.P. Dutton and Company, 1978.

Walker, Mary Alexander. *To Catch a Zombi*. New York: Atheneum, 1979.

Willard, Barbara. *The Lark and the Laurel*. New York: Harcourt, Brace, Jovanovich, 1970.

———— . *The Sprig of Broom*. New York: E.P. Dutton and Company, 1972.

———— . *A Cold Wind Blows*. New York: E.P. Dutton and Company, 1973.

———— . *The Iron Lily*. New York: E.P. Dutton and Company, 1974.

———— . *Harrow and Harvest*. New York: E.P. Dutton and Company, 1976.

———— . *The Miller's Boy*. New York: E.P. Dutton and Company, 1976.

Williams, Jeanne. *Winter Wheat*. New York: G.P. Putnam's Sons, 1975.

Young, Alida E. *Land of the Iron Dragon*. Garden City, N.Y.: Doubleday and Company, 1978.

Fantasy

Babbitt, Natalie. *The Eyes of the Amaryllis*. New York: Farrar, Straus and Giroux, 1977.

Bosse, Malcolm J. *Cave Beyond Time*. New York: Thomas Y. Crowell, 1980.

Bunting, Eve. *Ghost of Summer*. New York: Frederick Warne and Company, 1977.

Christopher, John. *Wild Jack*. New York: Macmillan Publishing Company, 1974.

DeLarrabeiti, Michael. *The Borribles*. New York: Macmillan Publishing Company, 1976.

Engdahl, Sylvia Louise. *Enchantress From the Stars*. New York: Atheneum, 1970.

———— . *The Far Side of Evil*. New York: Atheneum, 1971.

———— . *This Star Shall Abide*. New York: Atheneum, 1972.

———— . *Beyond the Tomorrow's Mountains*. New York: Atheneum, 1973.

Fisher, Leonard Everett. *Noonan*. Garden City, N.Y.: Doubleday and Company, 1978.

Hamilton, Virginia. *Dustland*. New York: Greenwillow Books, 1980.

Lawrence, Louise. *Star Lord*. New York: Harper and Row, 1978.

L'Engle, Madeleine. *A Swiftly Tilting Planet*. New York: Farrar, Straus, and Giroux, 1978.

Lightner, A. M. *The Space Gypsies*. New York: McGraw-Hill Book Company, 1974.

Mark, Jan. *The Ennead*. New York: Thomas Y. Crowell Company, 1978.

McCaffrey, Anne. *Dragon Song*. New York: Atheneum, 1976.

McHarque, Georges. *Stoneflight*. New York: Viking Press, 1975.

Moskin, Marietta D. *Dream Lake*. New York: Atheneum, 1981.

Naylor, Phyllis Reynolds. *Shadows on the Wall*. New York: Atheneum, 1980.

Selfridge, Oline G. *Trouble With Dragons*. Reading, Mass.: Addison-Wesley, 1978.

Sleator, William. *Among the Dolls*. New York: E.P. Dutton and Company, 1975.

———— . *The Green Futures of Tycho*. New York: E.P. Dutton and Company, 1981.

Snyder, Zilpha Keatley. *Below the Root*. New York: Atheneum, 1975.

———— . *And All Between*. New York: Atheneum, 1976.

———— . *Until the Celebration*. New York: Atheneum, 1977.

Westall, Robert. *The Wild Eye*. New York: William Morrow and Company, 1977.

Wiseman, David. *Jeremy Visick*. New York: Houghton Mifflin Company, 1981.

Appendix T*
Information about Authors and Illustrators

Addison-Wesley Series of First Person Picturebooks by Distinguished Illustrators.
  Zemach, Margot. *Self-Portrait: Margot Zemach*. Reading, Mass.: Addison-Wesley, 1978.
Doyle, Brian, ed. *The Who's Who of Children's Literature*. New York: Schocken Books, 1968.
Hoffman, Miriam, ed. *Authors and Illustrators of Children's Books*. New York: R.R. Bowker, 1972.
Hopkins, Lee Bennett. *Books Are by People*. New York: Citation Press, 1969.
———. *More Books by More People*. New York: Citation Press, 1974.
Junior Book of Authors Series. Bronx, N.Y.: H. W. Wilson.
  Kunitz, Stanley, ed. *Junior Book of Authors*. Up to 1951.
  Fuller, Mauries, ed. *More Junior Authors*. 1951–63.
  DeMontreu, Doris, ed. *Third Book of Junior Authors*. 1963–1972.
  ———. *Fourth Book of Junior Authors*. 1972–78.
Kirkpatrick, D. L. *Twentieth-Century Children's Writers*. New York: St. Martin's Press, 1978.
Ward, Martha. *Authors of Books for Young Children*. 2nd ed. New York: Scarecrow Press, 1971.
Wintle, John. *The Pied Pipers*. New York: Paddington Press, 1975.

*Lucille Lettow, Youth Librarian, University of Northern Iowa, provided information for this appendix.

Appendix U
Propaganda Techniques

Types of Propaganda Techniques

Bad Names

   Expressions with unpleasant connotations
   Examples:
   Dirty, coward, cheap, diseased, fat, communist

Glad Names

   Expressions with pleasant connotations
   Examples
   Clean, brave, exclusive, healthy, slim, All-American

Testimonial

   An affirmation of a person, theory, or thing
   Examples
   A well known athlete recommending a certain brand of athletic equipment
   The governor of the state supporting a particular candidate for the presidency
   A noted scientist supporting the building of a nuclear energy plant

Transfer

   Relating a highly regarded person, symbol, or concept to an idea or product that is being promoted
   Examples
   People accept ideas because research proves . . .
   An athlete endorsing cereal which is supposed to build strong bodies
   The American flag placed on writing tablets to promote sales

Plain Folk

   An attempt to involve the majority rather than an exclusive group
   Examples
   Politicians eating corn on the cob and chicken with their fingers, their wives reading *Good Housekeeping,* their children attending the public schools
   Average looking people, opposed to superglamorous ones, advertising products on television

Card Stacking

> Presentation of the best of one point of view and the worst of another point of view
>
> Examples
>> Woman explaining her car accident to her husband
>> Person explaining the defeat of the team supported in the game
>> Person explaining a poor report card

Band Wagon

> Involvement with the crowd
>
> Examples
>> Being modern
>> Being different
>> "Everybody's doing it"
>> The "in" thing
>> Slang

Strategies for Evaluating Propaganda

Analysis of Statements

> Are the statements true?
> Are the statements tricks? What techniques of propaganda were used?

Analysis of Speaker or Author

> Who is the propagandist?
>> Authority, reputation, knowledge
>
> What is the propagandist's purpose for giving the presentation?
> What is the viewpoint of the propagandist?
> What are the propagandist's biases?
> To what interests and emotions does the propagandist appeal?

Analysis of Self

> Is my mood or motivation for listening or reading interfering with comprehension?
> What are my biases?
> Are my opinions of the author interfering with comprehension?